IN PRAISE OF PROMETHEUS

IN PRAISE OF PROMETHEUS

HUMANISM AND RATIONALISM
IN AESCHYLEAN THOUGHT

BY LEON GOLDEN

THE UNIVERSITY OF NORTH CAROLINA PRESS · CHAPEL HILL

Copyright © 1962, 1964, 1966 by
The University of North Carolina Press
Manufactured in the United States of America
Library of Congress Catalog Card Number 66-19275
Printed by Kingsport Press, Inc.,
Kingsport, Tennessee

TO MY MOTHER AND FATHER

PREFACE

I WISH TO EXPRESS MY FEELINGS OF OBLIGATION AND GRATITUDE to individuals and institutions that have assisted, in general or specific ways, in the writing of this book.

I think, first, of two teachers, Benedict Einarson and Richard T. Bruère, who introduced me to the techniques of analysis and criticism of classical texts and set towering standards of achievement which still serve me as ultimate goals.

As sections of this book were written during my tenure on the faculty of the College of William and Mary, I wish to thank my many friends on that faculty for their encouragement and friendly interest in my work. I am under a very special and significant obligation to Frank Brooke Evans III, who, in many hours of general discussion about literary problems, as well as through critical scrutiny of sections of this manuscript, helped clarify a number of my ideas. I should like to thank the Committee on Faculty Research and the Administrative officers of the College of William and Mary for having provided me with several summer research grants which permitted the writing of sections of this book.

At various stages in the preparation of this book, I have received helpful assistance from Mr. James Servies, Librarian at the College of William and Mary, and members of his staff. The Harvard University libraries and staff several times generously accorded me privileges and courtesies that materially aided the completion of this project. In the concluding phase of my work Professor Cedric Whitman kindly checked certain matters for me in the papers of H. W. Smyth on deposit in the Harvard University library.

To the gifted students who contributed, sometimes consciously and sometimes unconsciously, to the development of my own ideas about human existence, tragedy, and Aeschylus I owe a debt of gratitude that I eagerly aspire to repay here.

This book was brought to completion with the assistance of a Fellowship in the Cooperative Program in the Humanities, a Ford Foundation project that is jointly administered by The University of North Carolina at Chapel Hill and Duke University. To the Ford Foundation, the Joint Supervising Committee of the Cooperative Program, and the staffs of the Departments of Classical Languages at The University of North Carolina at Chapel Hill and Duke University I express my deepest gratitude for assistance and courtesies extended throughout the year of my research grant. I wish, specifically, to thank Professor O. B. Hardison, Co-Chairman of the Joint Supervising Committee of the Cooperative Program, for the interest and aid he has given my project and also the late Professor Albert Suskin, Chairman of the Department of Classics at The University of North Carolina at Chapel Hill, who materially assisted my work by placing all of the facilities of his department at my disposal. I should also like to thank the Department's Secretary, Miss Nancy Honeycutt, for helpful assistance rendered in the typing of the manuscript.

The year of my research appointment fortunately coincided with the year in which Professor Franco Munari held a visiting professorship at The University of North Carolina at Chapel Hill. I owe to him many hours of stimulating conversation which helped me, in the important final stages of my research, to sharpen basic ideas and arguments. Sections of this book have benefited from a number of his suggestions and criticisms as well as his perceptive insight into the nuances of language and thought of ancient authors and modern scholars.

Sections of this book have appeared, in somewhat different form, in *Bucknell Review, Classical Philology, and The Transactions of the American Philological Association.* I wish to thank the editors of these journals for permission to use this material.

The interpretation of Aeschylus presented in the following pages will differ from that held by a number of very prominent contemporary scholars. If my arguments take strong exception to the points of view of Professors Lloyd-Jones, Page, and Solmsen they also are, in a very significant way, beneficiaries of the scholarly achievements of these men, and I am pleased to express my obligation to their work although, in my analysis and conclusions, I must take a very different path from them. I am particularly indebted to Professor Hugh Lloyd-Jones for the warm interest and encouragement he has given my work even when its basic conclusions differ widely from his.

This book is dedicated to my mother and father from whom I have learned essential lessons about life, the joy and the endurance of it, which are the only real subjects of Aeschylus or any poet.

CONTENTS

Preface		*vii*
One	THE INTERPRETATION OF AESCHYLUS	*3*
Two	PATRIOTIC DRAMA	*31*
Three	POLITICAL DRAMA I	*42*
Four	POLITICAL DRAMA II	*62*
Five	RELIGIOUS DRAMA	*100*
	CONCLUSION: THE ACHIEVEMENT OF AESCHYLUS	*127*
Bibliography		*129*
Index		*135*

IN PRAISE OF PROMETHEUS

CHAPTER ONE

THE INTERPRETATION OF AESCHYLUS

THE STUDY OF AESCHYLUS' POETIC ACHIEVEMENT IS CLOUDED over with severe and divisive controversy. Critics and scholars pay tribute to a genius who forged the essential structure of fifth century tragedy, a poet of excitingly rugged diction and vigorous imagination and an artist of deep religious commitment. An intuitive sense of the majesty of Aeschylus' art is shared by almost all who have seriously studied the poet but a grasp of the meaning of his work that can be accepted by a vast majority of Aeschylus' readers has not been achieved or even approached. Indeed, the interpretative disagreements that continue to rage concerning the meaning of the seven extant plays are of the most extreme and radical character. While the act of literary criticism, like the act of literary creation, is a subjective process which allows for various kinds and depths of views, and while a work of literature may legitimately be subject to varied interpretations, there are, nevertheless, limits of tolerance for divergent opinions about the meaning of any poet's work. Of Aeschylus it cannot *both* be true that "the faculty of acute or profound thought is not among his gifts" as

Professor Page states *and also*, as Professor Jaeger declares, that he

> ... took the main outlines of the character of Prometheus, the hero of the intellectual world, from Ionian theories of the origin of civilization, which with their triumphant faith in *progress* contrasted so sharply with the peasant Hesiod's melancholy description of the five ages of the degenerating world, and of its approaching ruin. Prometheus is inventive and exploratory genius, inspired by a helpful love for suffering humanity. ... In order to make Prometheus impart his enthusiasm to us as he does, *the poet must have shared in these lofty aspirations and himself admired the greatness of Prometheus' genius* [italics mine].[1]

Of Aeschylus it cannot *both* be true that "innumerable superstitions darkened and dominated the lives of men, even among the most intelligent; and in this respect Aeschylus was certainly not in advance of his time" as Page argues [2] *and also*, in Professor Dodds's words, that

> This haunted, oppressive atmosphere in which Aeschylus' characters move seems to us infinitely older than the clear air breathed by the men and gods of the *Iliad*. That is why Glotz [*Solidarité*, 408] called Aeschylus "ce revenant de Mycènes" (though he added that he was also a man of his own time); that is why a recent German writer [K. Deichgräber, *Gött. Nachr.*, 1940] asserts that he "revived the world of the daemons, and especially the evil daemons." *But to speak thus is in my view completely to misapprehend both Aeschylus' purpose and the religious climate of the age in which he lived* [italics mine]. Aeschylus did not have to revive the world of the daemons: it is the world into which he was born.[3] *And his purpose is not to lead his fellow-countrymen back into that world, but, on the contrary, to lead them through it and out of it* [italics mine]. This he sought to do, not like Euripides by casting doubt on its reality through intellectual and moral argument, but by showing it to be capable of a higher

1. For Page's view on this matter see his edition (with J. D. Denniston) of the *Agamemnon* (Oxford, 1957) p. xv. For Jaeger's view see the detailed quotation in note 9 below.
2. *Ibid.*, p. xiv.
3. Page cites this sentence (*ibid.*, p. xiv, n. 1) but strangely not the one which follows and which represents a direct contradiction of his thesis.

interpretation, and, in the *Eumenides,* by showing it transformed through Athena's agency into the new world of rational justice.[4]

In a religious poet's world view religious beliefs are all-important and until we can come to some understanding and agreement on Aeschylus' basic articles of faith we will be unable to claim that we really understand him.

Profound differences of opinion about philosophical outlook are complemented by strong disagreements about Aeschylus' technical skill as a playwright. Aeschylus cannot be both the inept craftsman Wilamowitz describes at work in certain plays[5] and the skillful poet, pictured in this book, who always molds the external form of his dramas to conform to their innermost spirit. The principal problem which, therefore, confronts the critic of Aeschylus is an overwhelming one—to provide a universally acceptable interpretation of the poet in the midst of a chaos of long-standing, often mutually exclusive, differences of opinion. A goal of such magnitude must be approached with due humility but approached it must be if any advance is to be made in our understanding of Aeschylus, and the richness of the ultimate reward justifies even failure if only it results from an honest attempt to meet the central issues squarely.

We must begin by attempting to set forth a rational, comprehensive, and consistent critical method. If we can accomplish this, we will have taken an important procedural step toward a truly significant interpretation of Aeschylus that will be, for all its necessary subjectivity, capable of validation by other readers of the poet.

The standards I shall now discuss are, I believe, quite self-evident but a restatement of them is necessary because they are

---

4. E. R. Dodds, *The Greeks and the Irrational* (Berkeley, 1951), p. 40.

5. Wilamowitz characterizes the *Persians* as "ohne jede Einheit der Handlung" and he accuses Aeschylus in the *Seven against Thebes* of constructing a disunified play out of "zwei ganz disharmonische Grundmotive." We will discuss these criticisms when we analyze the plays involved later in the book.

violated with surprising regularity in actual practice. The first requirement for any acceptable theory is that it be based upon adequate textual evidence and that this evidence be specifically cited for the benefit of those who wish to test and judge the stated hypothesis. Secondly, the evidence must be carefully weighed and balanced in regard to such considerations as its source, its tone, and its consistency with other lines of evidence within the play and, if possible and appropriate, in the poet's other plays. Here we must remember that a drama is not a disembodied text like a treatise of Aristotle. A line spoken by Clytemnestra, Mephistopheles, or Iago has a different weight than a line spoken by Cassandra, Faust, or Desdemona. Time and place, character and motive, and, above all, the cohesiveness of the total action of the play must be taken into consideration in weaving each individual piece of textual evidence into the fabric of a complete interpretation. As a third consideration, the theory must explain all important phenomena; it must not ignore or reject by fiat any evidence that significantly affects its validity. A fourth and connected point is that the theory must explain the cited evidence, like theories in the natural sciences, with simplicity and with the application of accepted methods of reasoning and analysis. A literary theory, like a scientific theory, loses strength in direct proportion to the number of *ad hoc* premises and unique assumptions it requires. Finally, the general interpretation expressed in the theory must be shown to be in harmony with what might reasonably be expected of the particular poet concerned writing under the specific circumstances of history and culture that actually prevailed. To sum up, a persuasive literary theory must be anchored to a bedrock of supporting textual evidence that is interpreted with appropriate sophistication and subtlety; it must explain phenomena in accordance with the normal rules of logic and in as simple and direct a manner as is possible; and it must show that the general interpretation that is finally arrived at is in harmony with the poet's cultural traditions and historical circumstances. If the above are taken as an acceptable set of standards for a literary theory then an interpretation that conforms to them can be given greater weight than one that violates them. Any new interpretation in this book will be justified, therefore, on the basis that it meets the requirements set forth above while any existing interpretation will be rejected on the basis that it fails to cite supporting textual evidence, that it fails to assess and interpret this evidence properly, that it violates the normal rules of reasoning, or that it is inconsistent with historical and cultural realities and probabilities. In a number of the necessarily polemical sections of this book, where radical disagreements in interpretation are involved, it will be argued that errors of the type just described, mainly through arguments by fiat or from authority, have been committed.

We may now move on from a consideration of literary theories in general to a discussion of specific theories that significantly influence our contemporary view of Aeschylus. Here we wish to restrict ourselves to a discussion of certain of the formal considerations which we discussed above as they apply to these widely disseminated and influential theories. In the succeeding chapters of this book we will present our own interpretations of individual dramas and of Aeschylus' work as a whole.

We have already indicated that the critical question in Aeschylean criticism is to define the poet's religious outlook. We have cited interpretations of Aeschylus' religious position that are in polar opposition and any advance in understanding the poet's work is dependent upon our either removing one of the contradictory poles or finding an acceptable intermediate ground between them. The basic thesis of this book contradicts certain important current interpretations of Aeschylus' religious position and so it is important to see if we can call into question any aspect of the critical method that was used to reach these interpretations. If we can, we shall have prepared the way for the attempt to supplant these views with those that are presented in the later chapters of this book.

The argument that Aeschylus is a naïve and backward religious thinker is supported essentially by two props. The first alleges a fervent Aeschylean belief in the Erinyes as a significant operating factor in the lives of men; the second asserts that Aeschylus envisioned a very primitive Zeus who bears witness to the poet's own religious naïveté and backwardness. Let us begin with the Erinyes. The thesis that the Erinyes play an important part in Aeschylus' theological outlook became a factor of the highest significance in modern Aeschylean criticism with the appearance of Friedrich Solmsen's article, "The Erinys in Aischylos' *Septem*," *TAPA*, LXVIII (1937), 197-211. This article has exerted a powerful influence on nearly all of the many scholars who have discussed the *Septem* in the three decades since it was written and its basic thesis has recently been applied by Professor Lloyd-Jones to an interpretation of the *Agamemnon* as well.[6] This thesis runs directly counter to the interpretation of Aeschylus' religious beliefs that will be presented in this book and so it becomes necessary to show the serious difficulties that I find in this view.

It is Solmsen's contention that the action of the *Septem* is determined by the intervention of the Erinys in Eteocles' fate. Under this interpretation, the play's meaning is intimately connected with the Erinys motif which Solmsen designates as the "*Leitmotif*" of the entire trilogy. If Aeschylus did intend the *Septem*, and the trilogy of which it is the final play, to illustrate the significant role of the Erinyes in human affairs then he clearly represents the primitive type of religious thought that Page and Lloyd-Jones have recently attributed to him since this would be a specific example of Aeschylus' affirmation that daemonic powers rule human events. Because many of those who have subsequently accepted this thesis have done so without rearguing the point or reassessing the evidence, the case for this position, as it has influenced modern scholarship, stands or falls on the strength of Solmsen's supporting arguments. We must, therefore, re-examine his position to see how strongly based it actually is. In the article

6. H. Lloyd-Jones, "The Guilt of Agamemnon," *Classical Quarterly*, XII (1962), 187-99.

cited above, Solmsen writes concerning the change in Eteocles' behavior which he sees taking place at 1. 653 ff. as follows:

In attempting to explain this change I prefer to be guided by Eteocles' own comments on his situation. In recent works there has been a tendency to read into the scene a struggle on the part of Eteocles to make up his mind and to decide between two alternative courses of action. Whatever one may think of the merits of this theory, it has certainly led some scholars to ignore the basic motif of the scene, namely the fact that the Erinys (or the Erinyes) who has been at rest in the former half of the play becomes once more active. The Erinys is the executor of Oidipus' ἀραί; she is, for this reason, included by Eteocles in his prayer (70). In 653 ff he awakes to the realization that his father's curse is coming to a head and that the Erinys is upon him, and it is this realisation which accounts for the emotional outbursts in 653 ff and later and for the change in his frame of mind which we have noticed. I think Eteocles' own utterances (655, 695 ff, 709 . . .) are definite enough to make any further proof unnecessary. It would, however, be unfair to Aischylos' religious feelings to regard these lines as irrelevant and to suggest that Eteocles is indulging in private hallucinations which to the poet himself mean little or nothing. The *Eumenides* shows how alive the Erinyes were and how important a place they had in Aischylos' religion. I suggest, therefore, that the coming into the play of the Erinys is the primary function of this scene and that the *onus probandi* devolves on those who assign to it a different function (pp. 198–99).

This passage which is a major part of Solmsen's argument that the Erinyes play an important role in Aeschylus' theological outlook can, I believe, be challenged on a number of important grounds. Solmsen's argument is actually based on the two statements quoted in the passage given above where he writes, "I prefer to be guided by Eteocles' own comments on his situation" and "I think Eteocles' own utterances . . . are definite enough to make any further proof unnecessary." There is a very important and unargued assumption here that Eteocles' views can be taken to represent, directly, those of Aeschylus. What are the grounds that justify this identification of Eteocles with Aeschylus? They can only be arguments that would show, on the basis of textual evidence, that Eteocles is meant to be the moral hero of the play and that the views presented here are consistent with the poet's religious world view as evidenced in his other work. Such argumentation is absent here and without this type of justification Solmsen's hypothesis remains unproved and unpersuasive. The Eteocles who is described in this book is anything but the moral hero of the play and if this interpretation is correct he most certainly does not represent Aeschylus' religious outlook but, rather, one that is totally rejected by the poet. The only way that this question can be settled is by a full citation and analysis of the relevant textual evidence for both conflicting opinions that can be assessed and judged by other critics. As the situation stands now, we must assert that although the Erinyes have been cited as a significant force in Aeschylus' theological outlook, no persuasive proof of this point has been given and until we have such proof we are free to entertain alternative hypotheses that seem better to fit our textual evidence. There are three other difficulties in Solmsen's argument here which must be mentioned. First, we have seen that on pp. 198–99 of the article from which we have quoted above, Solmsen has indicated that he accepts Eteocles' words as genuine indications of the actual situation in the play. On p. 200, however, in objecting to the belief of some critics that the *Septem* is concerned with Eteocles' patriotic decision to fight his brother, Solmsen writes: "No doubt there are passages in his passionate rejection of the chorus' warnings which may seem to support this interpretation—but only as long as we forget that the family curse is the central theme of the trilogy. Once this is remembered *the motives adduced by Eteocles himself in 684 ff and 717 become secondary in importance*" [italics mine]. If we are to accept Eteocles' words as proof of what is really going on in the play at one point but not at another then we are in a difficult, indeed impossible, situation especially when the passages that are accepted and rejected come from the same scenes. Solmsen needs to tell us what critical principles are at work that permit him to draw the distinctions he has made here before we can accept his argument as a valid interpretation of the meaning of the play.

Finally, we may add two points which, together with those discussed above, form the basis of the radical difference in interpretation that characterizes Solmsen's view and my own. In the passage quoted above Solmsen has argued that, "The *Eumenides* shows how alive the Erinyes were and how important a place they had in Aischylos' religion." Now we shall argue in this book that in the *Eumenides* we see the Erinyes enter into an agreement which puts an eternal limit on their power. First, they accept the verdict of the Areopagus and allow Orestes to go free, a situation they had vigorously and violently protested against earlier. We know that the Areopagus has been established "for all time" (ϵἰς ἅπαντ' ... χρόνον) and so the Erinyes in agreeing to stay in Athens and enjoy the gifts and powers Athena has bestowed upon them also tacitly agree to accept a kind of co-regency with a new force that has just set an important precedent in reversing their judgment and inhibiting their will. It is clear that this new force is expected to continue to act through all future time in a way that must often conflict with the principle of automatic blood vengeance that was the primary characteristic of the Erinyes' judicial philosophy before the volcanic issues of Orestes' matricide erupted and demanded a new solution. The authority for dealing with homicide cases under the new dispensation will belong to the Areopagus who are invited by Athena in the *Eumenides* to weigh and balance evidence, to seek into the questions of causation and motivation, in short, to use their full rationality in assessing the complex question of innocence and guilt rather than to apply, as an automatic response in each and every situation, a traditional principle of vengeance. If the Erinyes are "real" in the *Eumenides* then so is the Areopagus "real" and the action of that play shows us that Aeschylus believed, and publicly proclaimed his belief in the climactic work of his career, that the power of the Erinyes at one far distant point in the development of society had been eclipsed by the power of reason with tremendously exciting and all-important consequences for the history of human civilization. We shall recognize in our discussion later in this book, of course, that the Erinyes are retained with important powers in the state even after the Areopagus has been created. In our interpretation this symbolizes the fact that they represent an important and necessary element in all political situations, primitive or highly civilized, a deeply felt fear of the law's capacity for vengeance. Yet because of the prominent place now accorded the Areopagus we shall contend that it is clearly Aeschylus' opinion that whatever may have been the case in the early stages of human society, it is human reason that has been responsible for the development of civilization and which does and must govern its future progress. This picture of Aeschylus as a priest of the cult of rationality, it will be argued, harmonizes with other lines of evidence in the poet's work, notably with those from the *Prometheus Bound*, to provide the basis for a consistent and sophisticated world view. Thus the Erinyes are not presented by Aeschylus as the ultimate principle of justice in the world. Rather, they symbolize for him powerful and necessary social forces that have been tamed and altered in the course of history by the true organizing principle of our civilization, human reason. Later in this book we will attempt to explain the references to the Erinyes that Solmsen cites in a very different way that is consistent with the analysis that has been given above. There we will discuss them, as we believe they must be discussed, in the context of the character of Eteocles and the chorus, the two figures who refer to them in the *Septem*.

The last point on which I feel I must express my disagreement with Solmsen relates to the following statement (p. 199) in the article that I have already cited: "The Erinys brings Oidipus' curse to a head and the Erinys-motif provides a connection between the third play and the preceding two. Without it there would be only a continuity of subject; with it there is a continuity of idea and *Leitmotif*. Aischylos certainly constructed the plot of the *Septem* with the *Leitmotif* of the whole trilogy in mind, though he deliberately retarded the

Erinys' operation and allowed us to forget her for a while." Here we must object that a "*Leitmotif*" has been assumed without adequate argument. Since we have only very meager fragments from the other plays of the trilogy and since the argument about "*Leitmotif*" must hinge heavily on interpreted evidence from the *Septem* it is necessary that the supporting evidence be given in full. To say anything really certain about a lost play of a trilogy on the basis of an extant one is fraught with difficulties as can readily be seen from the problems that would face a critic who, if only the last play of the *Oresteia* had survived, would attempt to reconstruct the first one from it. If a rigorous proof that cites and analyzes supporting evidence is not given, then to posit the Erinys as the *Leitmotif* of the trilogy, and to infer from this what the meaning of the *Septem* must be, is a circular argument that lacks persuasion.

The second prop on which the contention that Aeschylus was a naïve and backward religious thinker has been based is the role Zeus is alleged to play in his work. We have seen that Page sees Aeschylus as a poet who accepted the "innumerable superstitions" that "darkened and dominated the lives of men, even among the most intelligent." We have already quoted Dodds to show that the matter is subject to widely divergent interpretations. In this book we shall dispute Page's interpretation on the grounds that an analysis of textual evidence not only fails to support his thesis but, indeed, provides the strongest possible justification for the contradictory point of view that is suggested by Dodds. With this problem as with all other major problems of interpretation radical disagreements can be resolved only by a full and explicit statement of the textual evidence on which judgments are made and a clear and careful exposition and justification of the inferences drawn from the evidence cited. Then, at least, objective observers can judge the merits of rival theses.

As we have already noted, in Aeschylean scholarship differences of opinion about intellectual outlook have their reflection in differences of opinion about the poet's technical skill. Although this problem is not of the same magnitude as that of the poet's religious and philosophical orientation it is related to it under the general heading of the poet's achievement and deserves mention here as it will be discussed on some occasions later in the book. In our analysis of the *Persians* and the *Septem* we shall be critical of efforts to praise or blame Aeschylus' technical skill which substitute a preconceived notion of what Aeschylus should or might have been trying to do for the attempt to discover, within the play, indications of the poet's essential intention that justify and, perhaps, necessitate the form that has been chosen. It has been possible for some important contemporary critics to assert that Aeschylus was a great poet but a naïve and backward religious thinker and, on some major occasions, an inept and rather stupid craftsman of his plays. Such a view makes a mockery of great poetry, which is nothing more nor less than a great vision that fires the human imagination, expressed by a greatness of technique that permits this vision to speak, eloquently and persuasively, to other men.

Up to this point we have attempted to indicate certain critical difficulties in the most important and influential interpretations of Aeschylus that are current today. In the following chapters of this book we shall argue for a very different interpretation of the poet's work on the basis of specific analyses of textual evidence. We must now attempt to set that part of our study on as strong a footing as possible by showing that the intellectual outlook attributed in it to Aeschylus developed logically and organically out of the intellectual and political environment of the age which produced and nurtured the poet.

This age is characterized by major developments in three significant areas of intellectual and political history. We note at this time the development of a national pride, a patriotism based on Athenian military and political achievements which is manifested and preserved for us in the art and literature of the fifth century; the development of social institutions with specific reference to the legal institutions on which an advanced society is based; and the impressive developments in intellectual history, centered about the pre-Socratic movement, with the scientific and technological advances it fostered which are of special importance for the present study.

Decisive events took place in the sixth century B.C. which paved the way for the brilliant role as a political and cultural leader which Athens played during the fifth century B.C. It is well known that under Pisistratus the social reforms instituted by Solon were extended and improved upon; economic and cultural progress were stimulated; and the rule of law was maintained by a benevolent tyranny. All of the intellectual, political, and material bases for the greatness of fifth-century Athens were visibly being assembled in the city of Pisistratus. During the sixth century, also, Persian power was growing and beginning to come into violent conflict with the Greek world. Thus Aeschylus was born into a city-state that was developing its cultural excellence and political significance. He was personally and significantly involved in the impressive Greek triumph over Persia which signaled the beginning of the period of the greatest Athenian cultural achievement. For the generation of Athenians born in 525 B.C. the developing political and cultural significance of their city was a marvelous and exciting condition of life. It should come as no surprise at all, then, that one of the main themes which runs through Aeschylus' work is a patriotic one in which the greatness of Athens, its past as well as its future glory, is praised with deeply felt emotion. In the *Persians* we will see a full play devoted to this theme and in a number of the other dramas we will find it present although subordinated to the broader and more universal intellectual interests of Aeschylus.

The century which preceded Aeschylus' birth was an age in which developments of the highest significance were made in the legal and social institutions of Athens. In the legal code attributed to Draco we find a revolution in the approach to the problem of homicide that bears a striking resemblance to the artistic treatment of the homicide theme in the *Eumenides*. The enduring contribution of Draco to the law of homicide consisted in replacing the demand for automatic vengeance for any murder, on the basis of religious considerations, with a more subtle and reasonable approach. In Draco's code we find provision made for refining the concept of homicide into its more precise elements such as premeditated, unpremeditated, and justifiable homicide. Suitable courts and appropriate punishments were set up for each subdivision of homicide. This process represents a clear victory of a rationalized system of justice over the primitive idea of automatic vengeance for any act of bloodshed. Professor Adcock's comments, quoted below, provide a striking connection between Draco's reforms and the theme we shall argue is the main one of the *Eumenides*. Adcock writes: "These laws of Draco are a skilful compromise between the claims of the family and of older religious ideas on the one hand and a more enlightened morality and more active intervention by the state on the other. They became a permanent part of Athenian jurisprudence and when Plato wrote his Laws he accepted for his model state the statutes which Draco had laid down for Athens." [7]

The tradition of rational improvement of the legal and political institutions of Athens continued, of course, from Solon through Cleisthenes into the lifetime of Aeschylus and serves as the second major theme which the history of his native city offered the poet as material for his art.

The third major environmental force that we must discuss as influential on Aeschylus' developing world view is the philosophical, scientific, and technological revolution that we associate with the pre-Socratic movement. In support of his thesis that Aeschylus is a naïve and backward poet, Page has urged that his work seems to come from an age much earlier than that of Xenophanes and Heracleitus. This judgment conflicts with evidence recently gathered by B. Gladigow and others and with the judgment of Werner Jaeger.[8] We have here another situation which can only be clarified by the full citation and analysis of the textual evidence on which strongly conflicting interpretations are based so that objective observers

---

7. F. E. Adcock, *Cambridge Ancient History* (Cambridge, 1960), IV, 31.

8. See B. Gladigow, "Aischylos und Heraklit," *Archiv für Geschichte der Philosophie*, N.S. XLIV (1962), 225–39. Gladigow refers to Werner Jaeger's supporting statement in *Die Theologie der frühen Griechischen Denker* (Stuttgart, 1953), p. 58.

can accept the more reasonable choice. We may emphasize
here that the view of Aeschylus as a rational humanist that is
presented in this book harmonizes closely with the conclusions
of Gladigow and Jaeger that link him to the progressive
intellectual movement of the sixth and fifth centuries B.C.[9]
Long before the development of more theoretical philoso-

---

[9]. We find comforting support for our view of Aeschylus' intellectual
outlook in a number of passages in the first volume of Werner Jaeger's
Paideia (New York, 1945). Jaeger writes as follows: "Aeschylus makes
him [Prometheus] not only a statesman but something of a sophist, as is
shown by the use of the word 'sophist' (which still had an honourable
meaning) in addresses to him. Palamedes too, in the lost drama of that
name, was depicted as a sophist. Both Prometheus and he proudly
enumerate the arts which they have discovered to aid mankind.
Prometheus is equipped with the newest geographical knowledge of
strange distant countries. In Aeschylus' time such knowledge was still
rare and mysterious, and stirred the eager imagination of the audience;
but in both *Prometheus Bound* and *Prometheus Unbound* the hero's long
lists of countries, rivers, and nations are not merely poetic decorations—
they demonstrate the omniscience of the wise Titan (252). . . . But
Aeschylus, with that mighty imaginative power which we cannot
sufficiently admire and honour, built up his [Prometheus'] act into an
imperishable symbol of humanity. Prometheus he made the Bringer of
Light to suffering mankind. The divine power of fire was for him the
concrete image of civilization. And Prometheus was the civilizing genius
who explores the whole world, who makes it subservient to his will by
organizing its forces, who reveals its treasures and establishes on a firm
basis the groping insecure life of man. Both Hermes, messenger of the
gods, and the spirit of sheer Force, servant of their justice, who rivets
the fetters on Prometheus, address him derisively as *sophist*, master of
discovery. Aeschylus took the main outlines of the character of
Prometheus, the hero of the intellectual world, from Ionian theories of
the origin of civilization, which with their triumphant faith in *progress*
contrasted so sharply with the peasant Hesiod's melancholy description
of the five ages of the degenerating world, and of its approaching ruin.
Prometheus is inventive and exploratory genius, inspired by a helpful
love for suffering humanity (262–63). . . . In order to make Prometheus
impart his enthusiasm to us as he does, the poet must have shared in
these lofty aspirations and himself admired the greatness of Prometheus'
genius. But he does not imagine that the work of a civilizing pioneer can
ever be crowned by one complete and glorious success. Again and again
the chorus repeats that the sovereign independence of creative genius
knows no bounds. Prometheus has separated himself from his brothers
the Titans and realized the hopelessness of their lives: for they recognize
no power but brute strength, and will not understand that the intellect
alone rules the world—that is how Prometheus conceives the superiority
of the new Olympian world-order over the Titans whom it has hurled
down to Tartarus (264)."

phy and science another great intellectual development had begun which lasted into Aeschylus' day, endures into our own, and will continue to exert its strong influence on human society as long as man populates the earth. This was the development of technology which was a principal agent in transforming primitive society into a civilized one. Here I should like to quote in some detail from Professor Farrington's study of Greek science to show the important stages in the development of ancient technology as seen by a modern historian of science. It will be of great interest, then, to compare this contemporary account with Aeschylus' view of the importance of technology in the advance of human society which we know from a famous passage in the *Prometheus Bound*.

The actual origin of civilization depended on the simultaneous mastery or possession of a number of techniques, some new, some old, which, taken together, sufficed to turn man from being mainly a food-gatherer into being mainly a producer of food. A permanent surplus of food is the necessary basis for the emergence of civil society. Then greater concentrations of population became possible, urban life began, and the neolithic village was overshadowed by the mighty town. The fundamental techniques were the domestication of animals, agriculture, horticulture, pottery, brickmaking, spinning, weaving, and metallurgy. These ways of imitating and co-operating with nature constitute a revolution in man's science and a revolution in his way of life. The first area where civilizations based on the combination of these techniques came into existence was in the Near East in the river valleys of the Nile, the Euphrates and the Indus. The vital period in which the new techniques were developed is roughly the two millennia from 6000 to 4000 B.C. . . .

Most techniques require at some stage the use of fire. Fire is a great teacher, man's greatest master in the art of chemistry. Pliny has a finely imaginative description of the rôle it has played in civilization (*Natural History*, xxxvi, 68). "I have now completed," he writes, "my description of the works of human ingenuity by which art imitates nature, and with great wonder I observe that fire is almost everywhere the active agent. Fire takes in sand and gives back, now glass, now silver, now minium, now various kinds of lead, now pigments, now medicines. By fire stones are melted into bronze, by fire iron is made and mastered, by fire gold is produced, by fire that stone is calcined which, in the form of cement, holds our houses over our heads. There are some things which it profits to submit more than once to the action of fire. The same original material becomes one thing at a first firing, another at a second, still another at a third. Coal itself, for example, begins to possess its strength only when extinguished, and when it might be thought to be exhausted its virtue is increased. O fire, thou measureless and implacable portion of nature, shall we rightly call thee destroyer or creator?" [10]

Anyone who compares these passages from Farrington's book with 1. 436 ff. of the *Prometheus Bound* must be struck by the similarity in tone and thought that he finds there. Through Farrington's historical account and Aeschylus' imaginative description there runs the same sense of enthusiastic affirmation of man's technological achievements and the catalogue of significant gifts—headed by that of fire, which Prometheus cites as his most significant benefaction of mankind—that bears a strikingly close relationship to the twentieth-century historian's list of necessary technological advances in the progress from primitive society to civilization. We can see that this emphasis on the significance of human technological progress, expressed by Aeschylus in the *Prometheus Bound*, harmonizes very well with the theme of the rational improvement of law and society which we have noted is central to the *Oresteia* and which plays a role in other plays.[11] The application of human

---

10. B. Farrington, *Greek Science* (Baltimore, 1953), pp. 17–18, 22.

11. An insight into the factors in Aeschylus' intellectual background that may well have been at work in bringing the poet to this unified world view is given by Jaeger, *Paideia*, pp. 142, 143–44. He writes:

With Ionian scientific ideas as a pattern, it was easier for Solon than for anyone before him to establish the fact that the political life of a community is subject to definite laws. He had as material for this induction the history of numerous Greek cities on both sides of the Aegean, in which during more than a century the same processes had run their course with remarkable uniformity. Because the political development of Athens started late, he was enabled to use the history of other states for his own prognosis, and by that educative act he earned his lasting fame. . . . Recognition of the universal truth that every

reason to the problems set by nature and society is the central theme of Aeschylean drama as, indeed, it was the central theme of human existence in fifth-century Athens. We hope, then, that we have adequately shown that the political and intellectual history of sixth- and fifth-century Athens provides a genuine basis for the interpretation of Aeschylus' work that has been suggested in this chapter and which will be developed further during the course of this book.

The Aeschylus who emerges from our analysis is a poet who is alive to the fundamental intellectual and political currents of his day as an active participant in the exciting achievements of his native city-state. He appears, in our view, as a poet who aligned himself with other fifth-century artists, philosophers, and political figures to soar above the past that bore them to create an ever-living, unique instant of perfection in the cultural history of man. As we have indicated, the type of poet he is and the causes for which he stands, under the interpretation we have given, clash violently with the picture of the poet that is currently standard. If we are to attain to a deeper understanding of Aeschylus then we must engage in an intensive effort to eliminate this wide difference of opinion that harbors within it mutually exclusive theses. This can only be done, as we have said, by a painstaking reassessment of all major interpretations of the poet in regard to the strength of the textual evidence and the validity of the logical inferences which support them. We hope that we have suggested earlier in this chapter suitable requirements and procedures for obtaining a more universally acceptable understanding of Aeschylus' achievement.

One very important factor, however, which is far more fundamental than plot or character or consistency of intellec-

---

community is bound by immanent laws implies that every man is a responsible moral agent with a duty to be done. Thus in Solon's world there is far less scope for the arbitrary interference of the gods than in the world of the *Iliad*; for it is governed by law, and attributes to the will of men many events which in the Homeric world were the gifts or inflictions of heaven. Accordingly, the gods merely carry into execution the effects of the moral order, which is identical with their will.

tual outlook, which were mentioned earlier as important considerations for a critic to investigate, needs to be discussed here. This is the question of how much we feel that a poet of a past age, such as Aeschylus, can really say that is relevant beyond his own era. It is important that we make explicit our intuitive assumptions on this point because they are powerfully influential in determining what we will expect or allow to be found in the text of an author. In other words, is Aeschylean drama a relic, an artifact, a museum piece of another era for which the critic's highest obligation is restoration, preservation and, perhaps, explanation of how it came to be what it was? Or is Aeschylean drama a triumph of humanistic achievement speaking, when understood correctly, a lordly and insightful message to all men at all times? The answer to this question involves a broader problem of the highest significance, the problem of the value, use, and relevance of art and literature in general, and of Classical art and literature in particular. Clarification of the axioms that govern a critic's approach to this problem will be a major step toward understanding and, hopefully, removing some of the most important sources of major interpretative disagreement in regard to Aeschylus. I shall attempt now to present, and defend, the axioms which govern the approach to Aeschylean drama and Classical literature that is found in this book.

Here we may profitably start with Aristotle. In a famous passage in chapter 9 of the *Poetics* he tells us that "poetry is more philosophical and more serious than history" and he explains that this is so because poetry is concerned with the universal while history is concerned with the particular. The universal is further defined as that which a certain kind of person would do or say according to probability or necessity. The artist in seeking to attain the universal expresses, if he is successful, a phenomenon of nature, and the only condition under which that would not have a contemporary relevance would be if qualitative differences can be shown to have arisen that totally separate the generations of civilized men from each other. Any one who believes that Classical literature is an artifact unconcerned with universal human experience is under obligation to demonstrate, rigorously, what the qualitative differences are that have emerged in basic human characteristics from antiquity to our own time. It is highly reassuring to the thesis of this book that a number of the greatest and most respected of modern Classical scholars have taken, as we shall show in some detail, a strong and eloquent stand in favor of the idea of an essential continuity of human experience from the Classical world to our own and have insisted upon the relevance of ancient thought and art to our contemporary situation. These scholars counsel us never to lose sight of the fact that the ultimate goal of all study of literature, ancient or modern, is to discover the essential humanistic significance, universal in application, of that literature. To do this many disciplines and techniques must be acquired but in literary study as in other disciplines the greatest of all sins is to mistake the necessary means for the ultimate ends. Scholars and critics who accept as their obligation the task of uncovering the universal element in ancient literature and communicating it to contemporary audiences will often be accused of reading "modern" ideas into an ancient text. From the argument that has developed so far it should be clear that the ideas we must be concerned with in our study of literature are neither "ancient" nor "modern" but, rather, the clearly universal ones. The prejudice, however, against seeing a modern relevance in such a poet as Aeschylus is so strongly expressed in much of contemporary scholarship and criticism that we feel it is important and necessary as support for the approach that is adopted in this book to cite certain general attitudes toward the study of ancient civilization from the writings of scholars whose authoritative achievements entitle them to a respectful hearing.

We have asserted the doctrine of the essential continuity of human experience as an axiomatic basis for approaching the study of ancient literature. This principle is used as a basis for understanding and interpretation in a historical context by Professor Gomme and since the reason for its use in both

instances is similar, if not identical, it will be of interest to
observe his argument. In a now famous and influential article
on "The Position of Women in Athens in the Fifth and Fourth
Centuries," Gomme wrote in strong opposition to existing
theories that dominated historical research at the time:

> . . . I consider it very doubtful if Greek theory and practice
> [in regard to the treatment of women] differed fundamentally
> from the average, say, prevailing in mediaeval and modern
> Europe. When Theognis said, "I hate a woman who gads
> about and neglects her home," I think he expressed a sentiment
> common to most people of all ages; and at least there were
> gadabouts for him to disapprove of. After all, a great deal of
> Greek literature deals with the relations between the sexes in
> one form or another; and it would have died long ago if Greek
> sentiments had been radically opposed to ours.[12]

It is hardly necessary to add our fullest agreement with
Gomme's last sentence and our belief that it is valid for all of
the themes of Greek literature that have lasted to our own
time. Gomme was, however, aware that this approach was
radically unacceptable to a number of scholars of his own day.
He describes a situation which the critic who searches for the
universal element in literature will find uncomfortably familiar:

> It is not difficult to recognize dramatic character in passages
> from books of our own time, when the whole books are
> known, just as we can guard ourselves against taking language
> too literally, and do not conclude from the existence of a
> women's corner in the newspaper that it necessarily follows
> that their interests are confined to subjects treated there, nor
> from the "Ladies' Enclosure" at Lord's that at the headquarters
> of cricket women are admitted indeed to the [games] but excluded from the sight of men; it is more difficult to be on our
> guard in dealing with ancient writings and fragments from
> them. But we have no right to suppose sententiousness in the
> place of dramatic propriety; to think that Euripides and
> Menander, any more than Jane Austen or Mr. Galsworthy,
> were not building up characters, but only felt inspired to add

12. A. W. Gomme, "The Position of Women in Athens in the Fifth
and Fourth Centuries," *Classical Philology*, XX (1925), 25.

their quota to man's proud store of knowledge as to the proper conduct and destiny of women. I shall not be believed, I know; I shall be told I am reading into the Greek a meaning which the author never intended; but that seems to me at least more intelligent than to suppose that such lines had no meaning at all.[13]

Gomme's remarks here and elsewhere in the article cited, even though he is not formally concerned with literature, are of the highest importance for the literary critic. Gomme demonstrates a sense of the universality of human experience and of the poet's methods and goals in representing character that is essential to understanding a work of literature. His assessment of faulty types of historical reasoning based on incomplete or inadequate analysis of evidence has its direct counterpart in the field of literary criticism and his method of dealing with a historical problem can serve as a useful example for the student of literature.

With Gomme's remarks as starting point and background, we may now conclude our task of supporting, as strongly as possible, the basic attitude toward Classical literature that lies at the heart of the critical point of view expressed in this book. Fundamental axioms in humanistic subjects, as in mathematics and the natural sciences, are not subject to demonstration. Their validity is determined by the meaningfulness of the results to which they lead. In literature and art the value of critical axioms lies in their capacity to make the artistic work yield its treasure of insight into the human condition. The fundamental axiom that states that all great literature is contemporary literature and ordains that the highest act of criticism is to recover the universally relevant from that literature has appealed strongly to a number of scholars whose achievements, like those of Gomme, give ample testimony to the soundness, sophistication, and legitimacy of their scholarly procedures. I shall cite now, at some length, statements drawn from the work of three such scholars although it is not to the authority of these men but rather to their insight and logic that I wish to appeal. These detailed citations are important for the

---

13. *Ibid.*, pp. 11–12.

argument of this book because they defend in the clearest, most eloquent, and strongest form the kind of approach to literature that I have attempted to apply in this study. It is my contention that acceptance of the doctrines expressed here, not only theoretically, but in the *actual practice of criticism*, will favor the interpretation of Aeschylus presented in this book as opposed to the interpretations which currently dominate Aeschylean scholarship and which operate, consciously or unconsciously, on the basis of very different theoretical principles. Our task will divide itself into three parts and for each of these parts we shall present, as supporting argument, the views of one of a very distinguished group of scholars.

First, on the most general and important level of the continuing relevance of Classical literature for contemporary life, I should like to cite certain remarks of Werner Jaeger that were written at a time, and under circumstances, that guarantee the deepest possible involvement in his subject:

The literature of the Greeks offers thus a splendid spectacle: the striving of the human spirit for the abiding expression of its ideals, the moulding of human excellence (its *arete*) from the heroic stage of the epic to the later phases of the tragic, the political, the philosophical man. The embodiment of these values in art was to be sure only what the Greek could create out of his Greek environment, and we have learned not to separate works of the spirit from their proper environment, as the older humanists did. We have learned to feel them more vividly and individually by referring them to the time and place and atmosphere of their origins. This does not mean however that we should see these works resolved into the history of their time and become merely sources for our knowledge of a bygone age. On the contrary the effort to grasp them in their first setting causes us to understand better how and why they had the strength to rise above their time into the regions of permanence and timelessness.

It is precisely this timelessness which history records. The revelation of heroic humanity in Homer did not seem antiquated to the Greeks of a later and more rational period. It maintained its validity far beyond a thousand years, and remained the foundation of culture through successive centuries of Greek life. In a similar way each new period made its contribution to that which the Greeks at the culminating point of their consciousness, in the fifth and fourth centuries before Christ, called their teaching, their lesson (*paideia*). Since they sought to mould the universal in the individual, in literature as well as in the plastic arts, their creative thought transcended the bounds of their own national existence, and in missionary spirit they early strove to extend their culture to other people. . . .

Thus even in antiquity the problem was propounded: to explain the mysterious circumstance that ideals and standards of excellence shaped under particular historical conditions by a particular people could maintain their validity and their inspiration for other times and other peoples, and become in fact human culture in a universal sense. Efforts will be made again and again to explain this quality of Greek culture and its Roman derivative. For us it is enough to know that it is so, and its truth is proven by the experience of the centuries since its origin.[14]

It is this view of Classical art and literature as a treasure house of universal experience and insight that motivates the type of analysis, whether it is successful or not, that is pursued in this book and which makes, in our opinion, the study of Classical civilization supremely rewarding and valuable.

If Classical literature is of the character that Jaeger described, then important consequences follow that affect the general world view of the classical scholar who would be the successful interpreter of this literature. The following words of E. R. Dodds express, explicitly and implicitly, requirements that must be met by any scholar who would seek to enhance, by his own work, Jaeger's vision of the place and mission of classical scholarship in the history of Western civilization:

What chiefly gives vitality to a man's teaching is not this or that small factual discovery, or even his joy in the process of

14. W. Jaeger, "Classical Philology and Humanism," *Transactions of the American Philological Association*, LXVII (1936), 371 ff. Jaeger's influence in regard to the conception of Classical Humanism has been great and beneficial. See, for example, O. Regenbogen's essay "Humanismus—heute?" in *Kleine Schriften* (München, 1961) pp. 463–79. This essay, like Jaeger's article that has been cited, bears an interesting and close relationship to the bitter and destructive political events which both scholars endured in their own lifetime.

such discovery, but rather his power continually to relive in his own person (and therefore not identically) a great experience in which other men have lived before him, to integrate the past with the present by making it a part of the living structure of his own mind. His originality is to set the past in a new and unique context, the new-born here-and-now; his creativeness, in the splendid phrase of Wilamowitz, is to lend his life-blood to the ghosts, that they may drink and live. This is plainly something above and beyond technique: it is the achievement of humanism. . . . What we can do, or attempt, is so to present the humanities that the poet, when God sends him, shall not find in them what Byron found, and many since Byron,
                    the daily drug that turned
          My sickening memory,
but may draw from them living sustenance and a stimulus to new creation.

Can we do so much? Housman thought not. Conscious, perhaps, that the future editor of Manilius and the author of *A Shropshire Lad* lived somewhat at odds in their common tenement, he insisted with emphasis that scholarship and taste were two things and not one. "In general," he says in the lecture already quoted, "if a man wants really penetrating judgements, really illuminating criticism on a classical author, he is ill advised if he goes to a classical scholar to get them." And he proceeds to point out that "the critics with real insight into the classical spirit" have not been professional scholars, but men like Lessing or Goethe or Matthew Arnold. . . . I find much the same view of Housman's expressed in a very interesting recent book by the President of Corpus. "The closest knowledge of the text," he says, "does not necessarily imply the deepest draught of the spirit. The scholar is indispensable to the understanding of the classics, but in a sense, he may never understand them himself." Scholarship, "though it performs the essential work of making vital appreciation of a civilization possible, is no more that appreciation than dogma is religion."

The history of classical scholarship since the eighteenth century lends much support to this description. That may be one reason why the classics hold to-day so insecure a place in our education. For this view seems to equate scholarship with technique; it conceives the scholar as a germ-carrier, unwittingly infecting others with an insight to which he is himself immune. This may be his traditional part; but if we value technique chiefly as a means to the dissemination of humanism, we may question the wisdom of employing blind men to scatter the seed, and may feel little surprise at the scantiness of the resulting harvest.[15]

Here Dodds has called for a broadness of scholarly perspective that justly matches the high significance Jaeger has attributed to the Classical tradition as a vital force in the continuing history of Western civilization. Having dealt with the universality and humanistic value of Classical studies and with the breadth of world view that is needed by the Classical scholar if he is to be an honest and effective interpreter of his subject, we have one final point to discuss that will bridge the distance from these more theoretical considerations to the specific area of criticism with which this book is concerned. The general spirit which animates the writings of Jaeger and Dodds is applied specifically to the literary domain by Professor Cherniss in a paper that is of overwhelming importance for anyone who seeks to understand the full meaning of Classical literature. The following passages indicate some of the principal judgments and insights offered by Cherniss in which we have found encouragement and inspiration but his entire discussion deserves to be read fully and with the greatest of care.

So we are brought back to the texts themselves. If, then, we can never appreciate them as the original audience did and if, again, the reconstruction of the author's biography cannot lead us to understand them, are we to say that true understanding of a work of art is impossible? Consider first, for a moment, what reason there could be for studying a work which had no meaning except for a single audience in a single spot at a single moment in the past! The historian interested in the nature of that audience might use such a work, but only as a means of understanding the audience and without concern for the work itself. Only a madman would even wish to transmute himself into a member of that audience in order to appreciate what could have no meaning for men at any other time or place. . . .

When one reads a poem of Sappho's and reads it as a poem, one is interested primarily neither in Sappho of Lesbos nor in

15. E. R. Dodds, *Humanism and Technique in Greek Studies*, (Oxford, 1936) pp. 10 ff.

the particular audience to which her poems were originally addressed; one has no desire to transmute himself into a member of her circle or to gather psychological data concerning the author, but one does expect to find the poem itself directly significant. That this expectation need not be futile is due solely to the fact that a work of art exists independently of its author and of the accidental circumstances of its production, that its artistic qualities are entirely contained within itself and are not to be explained by anything outside of the work. This alone is the reason that it can be understood and appreciated; it is only for this reason that it is worth considering at all, for this independent existence makes possible the direct approach of each individual to the work and makes this direct approach the only possible way of comprehension and appreciation. . . . The term "universal," so often applied to a work of art, means not that that work is not a unique individual, but that it has significance for all men as men in all times and places, and this, we saw, is a possibility only if the work has independent existence. But the basis of this universal significance is a set of ideas, emotions, and values which thus far in the history of the civilized world at least have always been recognized as having validity beyond the arbitrary taste of any individual or the customs of any locality. . . .

The insidious danger of the biographical method lies in its assumption that the essence is merely a combination of accidents, that literature is an automatic by-product of external forces, whence comes its tacit conclusion that no literary work has autonomous significance. Such an attitude will have fatal consequences for the study of the classics, for all justification of that study depends finally upon the value of the literary monuments of Greece and Rome, not their value as source books for the historian, the antiquarian, or the psychoanalyst, but their value for men as human beings. We pride ourselves mightily on our "true historical sense," of which, says one famous modern classicist, "Lessing and Gibbon had scarcely a notion, for they thought that man in all ages is essentially the same." Perhaps that is why the writings of Lessing and Gibbon can still be read with understanding today while the books of the new scholarship are antiquated after a decade. When the Hellenist no longer believes in man as *man*, he may as well shut his books, for he has confessed that he can never understand them.[16]

16. H. Cherniss, "The Biographical Fashion in Literary Criticism," *University of California Publications in Classical Philology*, XII (1933–44), 289 ff.

The separate gospels of Classical Humanism that Jaeger, Dodds, and Cherniss preach achieve a striking and eloquent harmony. Of the many links which bind together the views of these three scholars, one stands out as all-important. This is their respect for the relevance of the insights of Classical civilization for all men at all times. The acceptance or rejection of this great theme of universality determines, in a most important way, what one seeks and what one finds in the study of ancient civilization. The present study has made bold to set as its goal the uncovering of the universal relevance of the work of Aeschylus under the persuasion that classical scholarship is something more than a technique or an avocation but is, rather, as Jaeger, Dodds, and Cherniss argue, the priestly task of keeping and interpreting texts wherein are written transcendently important and illuminating insights into the nature of the human condition.

The search for the universal element of Aeschylean thought, in the spirit of the three great scholars from whom we have quoted at length, is the ultimate goal and justification of this study. It need hardly be added that because of limitations of knowledge and skill on the part of the author, the attempt made here may fall short of its goal. Should this be the case, still it is hoped that to have acted, no matter how inadequately, within the spirit of the great humanistic tradition, cannot be completely without value.

CHAPTER TWO

PATRIOTIC DRAMA

AESCHYLUS HONORS HIS NATIVE CITY OF ATHENS AT MANY POINTS in his work but only in the *Persians*, of the extant dramas, is the patriotic motif the dominant one. The play's unusual theme and form have caused severe difficulties for critics. Some [1] have interpreted its undoubtedly unique characteristics as structural defects which mar the play; others [2] admit the presence of certain structural inadequacies but find a saving grace in the play's epic or religious themes. Recently Professor Broadhead, the author of the most comprehensive edition of the *Persians*, has attempted to show that it is an adequate and perhaps superior work even when judged within the context of an Aristotelian concept of tragedy.[3]

1. See C. J. Blomfield, *Aeschyli Persae* (London, 1840), pp. xii-xiv; U. von Wilamowitz-Moellendorff, *Aischylos: Interpretationen* (Berlin, 1914), p. 48; H. D. F. Kitto, *Greek Tragedy* (London, 1950), p. 43.
2. See G. Murray, *Aeschylus: The Creator of Tragedy* (Oxford, 1940), pp. 111-30; H. W. Smyth, *Aeschylean Tragedy* (Berkeley, 1924), pp. 64-91; P. Groeneboom, *Aischylos' Perser* (Göttingen, 1960), pp. 13-14.
3. H. D. Broadhead, *The Persae of Aeschylus* (Cambridge, 1960), pp. xv-xlviii.

The battleground for these divergent critical opinions has been character portrayal and plot development. It will be instructive to see the widely disagreeing critical opinions that have been held on these subjects and then to determine whether it is possible to adjudicate these differences through a renewed study of the text. In regard to the depiction of character Sidgwick tells us that in this play Aeschylus "neither succeeds nor fails; for he does not attempt it."[4] Broadhead remarks: "Our study of the characters, then, leaves us with the strong impression that the dramatist has sought to delineate, not with prejudice or malice, but with sympathetic imagination, the Persian tragedy as he conceived it to have affected the Persian people, and, in particular, the ruling class."[5] In regard to the plot of the play Wilamowitz stated: "Thus the drama presents three, in actuality, independent acts, in which the effect of the defeat on the Persian people is expressed in essentially lyrical terms. The play is composed, to be sure, by a born dramatic writer, who understands how to produce tragic emotion and scenically effective images in each act. However, he has not yet achieved the unity of action. It is very much worth noting that in 472 Aeschylus could still construct a tragedy without any unity of action."[6] Broadhead, disagreeing radically, writes:

> In spite of such structural looseness, however, the *Persae* is far from lacking unity, and this unity derives partly from the omnipresent emotional tension, from the foreboding and anxiety of the πάροδος and first ἐπεισόδιον to the dejection, despair and humiliation of the later scenes, partly from the fundamental idea round which the tragedy is built—the punishment of ὕβρις by the divine powers—and partly from the recurring insistence that Xerxes is the prime cause of the tragedy. All these strands are closely interwoven, and provide an inner bond linking scene with scene.[7]

4. A. Sidgwick, *Aeschylus: Persae* (Oxford, 1903), p. xi.
5. Broadhead, *The Persae of Aeschylus*, p. xxix.
6. Wilamowitz, *Interpretationen*, p. 48.
7. Broadhead, *The Persae of Aeschylus*, p. xl.

Atossa figures significantly in the scholarly disagreements about the nature of character development in this play. This disagreement is clearly seen from Sidgwick's comment that "she is depicted simply as an anxious, superstitious, ignorant woman. . . ."[8] and Broadhead's remark that "she strikes us as the most freshly drawn of the *dramatis personae*, distinguished above all for her queenly dignity and her intense devotion to her son. . . ."[9] Although Broadhead has asserted the existence of certain positive qualities in the character of Atossa, he fails to give references to the text that support his interpretation. In fact, his own commentary in various places appears to undercut his basic thesis. A few lines after making the statement quoted above, he calls Atossa's role in the messenger scene a "largely formal one" and adds that "neither in her questions nor in her comments is there anything specially characteristic." A little later in commenting on Atossa's reaction to the story of Psyttaleia, he says, "one feels that in this part of the play the characterisation is unconvincing." The text here amply justifies his judgment. In Atossa's next appearance (ll. 598 ff.) after the scene referred to above she simply indicates her intention to sacrifice to the gods of the lower world. Broadhead does not indicate, and the text does not justify, an interpretation of her character here in terms of psychological depth or sophistication. Atossa's conversation with the ghost of Darius (ll. 709 ff.) also is basically informational and does not probe the queen's character. Her final appearance (ll. 845 ff.) in which she laments her son's wretched fate and goes to bring him decent clothes to wear is like her other statements, basically narrative, and reveals no perceptive insight into her character. Thus the text, itself, and some of Broadhead's own comments seem to contradict his interpretation of Atossa as "the most freshly drawn of the *dramatis personae*."

In regard to Darius the same violent critical disagreement exists. Sidgwick notes as one of the indications that this play is

8. Sidgwick, *Aeschylus: Persae*, p. x.
9. Broadhead, *The Persae of Aeschylus*, p. xxvi.

primitive in structure "the strange condition of mind which the dead Dareios exhibits . . . ,"[10] whereas Broadhead asserts that Darius is an "imposing, dignified and majestic figure" who "heroic in stature . . . regarded almost as a god . . . has the commanding presence of an Olympian deity."[11] Yet again textual evidence for his interpretation is lacking. In his entire appearance Darius merely asks for and gives information and utters some pious but obvious comments and warnings about Xerxes' conduct. Nothing Darius says or does provides any penetrating insight into his thought or character, and Broadhead fails to analyze Darius' lines to support his opinion quoted above.

There is less disagreement about the other characters in the play. The chorus plays a traditional and extensive role, and the messenger fulfills an obviously informational and narrative one. It is generally agreed that Xerxes' function is to heighten the pathos of the Persian defeat although there is some dispute about whether Aeschylus meant also to ridicule him in portraying his return home in rags. It is, however, clear that Xerxes is in no sense a fully drawn character, but is merely a vehicle for expressing a somber and protracted lament for the disaster he has caused.

In our survey of characterization we have seen that the *Persians* has no figures of the stature or complexity of Agamemnon, Clytemnestra, Prometheus, or Eteocles. Sidgwick's judgment that Aeschylus does not attempt character drawing here seems amply justified. The characters are merely the poet's means for announcing, commenting on, and lamenting the disasters that have befallen the Persian army. We are never introduced to their personal qualities or their complexity as individuals; all the poet permits us to see of them is their relation to the cataclysmic events now burdening the nation. The messenger announces these events, and the chorus laments them as a principal party to the suffering of the state. Atossa's role in the action heightens the pitiable situation since she has

10. Sidgwick, *Aeschylus: Persae*, p. x.
11. Broadhead, *The Persae of Aeschylus*, p. xxviii.

shared the glory of Darius' rule and must now witness the abject defeat of her son. We note that her principal concern in regard to Xerxes is for his torn garments, which are a symbol of the sunken dignity of the Persian state. In these extreme circumstances, if Aeschylus had meant to draw Atossa realistically in the role of a mother, many other considerations would have been more appropriate for her to comment on than the condition of the clothes her son wears on his return. Nor is Darius' appearance accompanied by a penetrating study of his relationships as husband and father. He praises the glorious leaders of the past, chides his son for arrogance, and warns Persia not to advance across the sea to Greece again. His appearance, like Atossa's, emphasizes the fall from greatness in Xerxes' defeat. His lament for the destruction of Persian greatness makes us focus our attention on the political and military defeat of a once great nation and not on any personal relationships existing between Darius and the other characters in the play. Xerxes' appearance in the final scene can be characterized only as pure lament, a groaning testimonial of personal grief and guilt openly expressed by one who has seen his own arrogant folly as the cause of the disaster that has befallen his country. We may, therefore, conclude that the characters in this play exist simply as vehicles for the expression of lament, grief, and recrimination. The drawing of character in the *Persians*, then, is unique in the corpus of Aeschylean writings since in all the other plays, including the *Suppliants*, a more detailed and complex characterization of the principal figures is given.

The second major characteristic of the *Persians* that makes it a source of critical contention is the nature of its plot. Broadhead, recognizing the exceptional quality of the plot, attempts to defend it as follows: "In short, the *Persae* is virtually devoid of the 'action' characteristic of a gradually developing 'plot'; but, inasmuch as the nature of the subject and the limitations it imposed made such a plot aesthetically undesirable, it was practically inevitable that a tragedy dealing with the Persian defeat should consist largely of scenes that depicted effects instead of actions that led to a reversal of fortune."[12] Yet Broadhead's defense cannot explain away the absence of one central characteristic which lies at the heart of all drama and yet is strangely lacking in this one. In this play, as Sidgwick notes, the conflict or *agon* which is of central importance in all other Aeschylean plays, including the *Suppliants*, is completely missing. Conflict of some sort is the heart and soul of drama as we regularly find it, and the absence of this element in the *Persians* is a strong indication that it has not been designed to fit the traditional mold. The conflict upon which this play turns has long since been over, and the play itself represents a ceaseless and pitiable lament for what has occurred. Atossa, Darius, Xerxes, and the chorus are passive sufferers, not active agents in conflict with an adversary.

We have seen that in the *Persians* character development is minimal and rudimentary, that conflict is completely missing from it, and that the purpose of all elements of the drama is to convey a mood of grief and lament which could not fail to have stirred an Athenian audience that had experienced the great Pan-Hellenic struggle against Persia a few years before. We have noted that previous criticism of this play found it either primitive and inadequate in structure or attempted to force the facts of the play violently into a scheme for which textual evidence is lacking. It may be that the attempt to understand the *Persians* in terms of traditional tragedies is mistaken and that its unique qualities require us to establish a different and nontraditional critical standard for dealing with it.

I think that we must assume, first, that the creator of the *Oresteia* and the *Prometheus Bound* did not produce the effects found in the *Persians* through immaturity or incompetence.[13] The lack of character delineation and the introduction of a plot lacking conflict are so radically opposed to the traditional requirements of tragedy that they must have been

---

12. *Ibid.*, p. xxxv.
13. At the time of the writing of the *Persians*, Aeschylus would have been fifty-three years old. The play, therefore, cannot be dismissed as the work of a tyro.

consciously intended by the poet. If this is so, it is clear that Aeschylus in this play did not propose to write a traditional drama but something very different. Nearly all critics would agree that the basic achievement of the *Persians* is the evocation of a mood of lament and grief that serves, far more than plot and character, as the source of the most vivid and lasting impressions that a reader gains from the play. So important is the element of lament that some critics have described the play as having epic or lyric rather than dramatic qualities. Structurally, then, the action of the *Persians* consists of a narration of relevant events, praise of the dead Darius and his rule, and a long lament for the misfortunes caused by Xerxes' arrogance. We may well consider what possible influences were at work molding the form of a play constructed on such unusual principles.

There is in Greek literature another literary genre which came into prominence at about the time the *Persians* was written and which has a number of elements analogous to those in this play. This literary genre is that form of epideictic oratory known as the funeral oration. In speaking of epideictic oratory Professor George Kennedy, in his recent study of Greek rhetoric, remarks:

> More generally these speeches are classed as *epideixeis*, or demonstrations, and the genre is called epideictic. According to Aristotle (*Rhetoric* 1358 b 2 ff.) they are addressed to spectators, who are concerned with the ability of the speaker, not to judges; they deal mostly with the present, though they may recall the past or anticipate the future; their end is usually the demonstration of the honorable or disgraceful, and they are adapted to being read as well as being heard by the exactness and detail of the style (1414 a 18). Aristotle clearly thinks of epideictic as a speech or pamphlet written to praise or vilify someone or something. The *Rhetorica ad Alexandrum* speaks of the species of praise and blame rather than the genus of epideictic, though such speeches are delivered "not for the sake of contest, but of demonstration" (1440 b 13). The subdivisions of epideictic recognized in later antiquity, for example, panegyric, encomium, invective, and funeral oration, are all concerned with praising or blaming. . . . Epideictic is

the form of oratory closest in style and function to poetry; both epic and drama are also delivered before spectators rather than before judges of fact or policy. There is no intrinsic reason why the content of epideictic could not be as profound as the content of tragedy. In later antiquity, when the victory of rhetoric in literature was complete, virtually all poetry was regarded as a subdivision of epideictic.[14]

I have quoted Kennedy in detail in order to show the close relationship between poetry and epideictic oratory. He also notes that the introduction of the funeral oration as a prominent literary genre has been dated either at the time of the Persian Wars or, under the direction of Cimon, in 475 B.C., some three years before the original presentation of the *Persians*.[15] Either date would be sufficiently close in time to the writing of the play to establish at least the possibility of influence. Kennedy tells us that according to the later rhetoricians the structure of the funeral oration consisted of three parts: praise, lament, and consolation. The most famous funeral oration in antiquity, that of Pericles, has these three elements. In Pericles' oration praise is divided between the nation's long-honored dead and those whose recent death is the occasion of the present speech. This praise is coupled with a general eulogy of the state and the greatness that develops

14. G. Kennedy, *The Art of Persuasion in Greece* (Princeton, 1963), pp. 152-53.

15. See Kennedy, p. 154. The close relationship between poetic laments and funeral oratory is discussed by T. C. Burgess, *Epideictic Literature* (Chicago, 1902), pp. 146-47. He says, "The θρῆνος of Homer . . . and the later poets . . . represented the same qualities of human nature, but expressed in a far more natural and spontaneous manner. No one can doubt the direct connection between the poetic and the later prose lament as it appears in the public and private ἐπιτάφιοι. But the transition lies in the misty period preceding the sixth century and cannot be observed. Snell (ed. Lysias' *Epitaphios*, p. 9) says: 'The cause of the transformation of the *threnos* into the *epitaphios* must be sought in the altered state of society at Athens toward the close of the sixth century.' He mentions the growth of oratory and the general state of enthusiasm so prominent after the Persian wars as main factors. The ἐπιτάφιος as an annual solemnity seems to have arisen not long after the victory over Persia." For the relationship between the primitive Greek *threnos* and the choral odes of lament in the *Persians* see R. Hölzle, *Zum Aufbau der lyrischen Partien des Aischylos* (Marbach a.N., 1934), pp. 12 ff.

from, but greatly transcends, the heroism of its individual citizens. There follow a brief lament for the dead (which is more an argument against the propriety of lamenting those who have so nobly died) and then a note of consolation for the parents and relatives of the dead. The speech ends with the words, "and now, when you have lamented whomever it is fitting for each to lament, depart" indicating that the period of mourning is over and a courageous rededication to life is to begin. There is also at the beginning of the speech a brief narration of the circumstances leading up to the giving of the oration. The greatest part of the speech is devoted to the element of praise, the smallest to lament, and a very moderate part of it to consolation. This is a highly appropriate arrangement in view of the circumstances under which the speech was given. The oration honored the death of those who fought to defend a state held in reverence and awe. It is spoken at a moment of pride in the achievements of Athens, with full belief in the justice of its cause, and with confidence in eventual victory. Since it is my contention that the *Persians* bears a similarity in thematic structure to a funeral oration, let us now compare its thematic elements with those of Pericles' speech. In the *Persians* the first quarter of the play describes the circumstances surrounding the expedition Xerxes led against Greece. Nearly all the rest of the play is devoted to a grief-stricken recounting and lament over the disaster that has overtaken the state. There are brief sections of praise for Darius and the prosperity of the state under him but no consolation whatsoever is offered as the play ends with the chorus' line, "I shall escort you with the grim sound of lament," indicating that ceaseless grief, arising from total defeat, is the Persian heritage for their ill-conceived venture against Greece. The historical circumstances of the writing of the *Persians* explain this arrangement of thematic materials in the play. The *Persians* represents a defeated enemy's reaction to its shameful fate as that reaction is *imagined* by a poet of the victorious side. Since the historical situation presented in the *Persians* is, in many ways, the reverse of what we found in

Pericles' funeral oration, the thematic elements of the play, although essentially the same as those of the speech, are very differently arranged in it. The element of praise is found in the *Persians*, but only in regard to Darius, and is used to set off the folly of Xerxes and to emphasize the pain of defeat for a nation that had known much better days. The ceaseless, grim lament in which nearly the entire play consists is also highly appropriate for this play since this is exactly what a victorious Greek poet and his audience might proudly imagine as the state of mind of an enemy who was severely defeated in an attempt to conquer them. For the same reason the absence of any note of consolation is as well suited to the *Persians* as the emphasis on praise and consolation is highly appropriate in Pericles' funeral oration. If a Persian statesman had pronounced a funeral oration at the end of the Persian Wars, it would have been reasonable to an exulting Greek audience for him to follow the formula set down in the *Persians*. There would be praise for the happier days under Darius, a long lament for the terrible losses suffered by the state, and no real ground for hope or consolation. It is my argument, then, that the *Persians* bears a close thematic resemblance to a funeral oration and that, when it is interpreted with this relationship in mind, it achieves a satisfactory artistic unity and significance. We have now mentioned the thematic similarities between the *Persians* and funeral oratory and we have cited evidence showing that the rise of the funeral oration as a prominent genre coincided with the period in which the *Persians* was written. Because of these thematic and chronological connections I suggest that the *Persians* is a unique kind of tragedy that is related in spirit to epideictic oratory, the parent genre of the funeral oration. The play is a tragedy because it portrays the pitiful and fearful events that are the subjects of all tragedies. However, it is a unique form of tragedy that I would like to call epideictic, since its object is not to achieve the aesthetic-intellectual goals which Aristotle attributes to traditional poetic tragedy but rather to *praise* or, in this case, to *condemn* the qualities of spirit or mind that led to the pitiful and fearful events depicted. The *Persians* is the only extant drama of this kind, although Phrynichus' *Capture of Miletus* and *Phoenissae* also may very well have belonged to this category. We may conjecture that epideictic tragedy failed to achieve great prominence in antiquity since its methods and goals were far more suited to formal rhetoric than to poetry.

The advantage that we draw from recognizing the *Persians* as an example of epideictic tragedy is that we are no longer required to force its plot and characterization into an Aristotelian framework for which they were never designed and which they poorly fit. Moreover, we need no longer worry about deviations from historical accuracy and realism in the text since we are dealing with a work which enjoys a rhetorical license to mold history to its special purposes.[16] As with all examples of epideictic literature we cannot be expected to muster as much enthusiasm for it as those who were contemporary with the events described, but we can now at least judge it on its own, and not on alien terms. Although the *Persians* suffers from this limitation, it has an important value for our study of Aeschylus' world view since we find in this play the clearest and fullest expression of the patriotic theme which has softer but quite distinct echoes throughout the poet's work.

We should be grateful that Aeschylus, obeying his true genius, turned his most constant and productive attention on poetic rather than rhetorical subjects. For all the intense popularity we can imagine they once enjoyed, Atossa, Darius, and Xerxes have become little more than artifacts of literary history for us, whereas Agamemnon, Clytemnestra, and Prometheus have attained a vital significance in the literature and thought of Western man. Between Aeschylus' major works and the *Persians* there lies the vast aesthetic chasm that separates the rich universality of the poetic from the pale transience of epideictic tragedy.

16. Aeschylus' distortions of history are discussed by R. Lattimore, "Aeschylus on the Defeat of Xerxes," in *Classical Studies in Honor of William Abbott Oldfather* (Urbana, 1943), pp. 82–93.

CHAPTER THREE

POLITICAL DRAMA I

IN THE *Suppliants* AND THE *Seven against Thebes* POLITICAL themes play a dominant role. Since the former play is the first one in a trilogy whose subsequent development cannot be traced with certainty, our only firm clue as to its ultimate significance must come from an examination of the development of its most prominent theme.

Central to the action of the *Suppliants* is the attempt of the Egyptians to impose their will upon the Danaids without regard to any higher consideration of law or morality. Throughout the play the Egyptians are characterized by violent, arrogant, and contemptuous behavior which drives the Danaids to threaten at 1. 872 ff. to defend themselves through suicide on sacred ground, a course of action that would bring extreme pollution on the Argive state. The Egyptians' surly threat of violence, evoking from the Danaids this counter threat which could destroy the people to whom they have come as suppliants, places the Argive king squarely in the center of a very tense situation. In trying circumstances, his recourse is not to use force to settle the problems raised by force but rather to consult the will of his people who are advised of the moral as well as political and military aspects of the situation they face. The action of the Argive king in consulting his people, symbolic of democratic practice such as Athens boasted, is sharply contrasted with the brute physical violence of the Egyptians. Thus there is a tension in this play between the rule of law, deriving one sanction from the will of the people and a higher one from an appeal to religious and moral considerations, and the arrogant and defiant assertion of personal will and desire as the crowning principle of human action. We cannot say, because of the lack of evidence for the final plays of the trilogy, exactly how Aeschylus worked this political motif into the thematic significance of the trilogy as a whole. We can, however, see his treatment of this question here as an earlier and preparatory step leading to the more detailed analysis of the problem which appears in the *Seven against Thebes*. The *Seven*, itself, is a connecting bridge to the expression of Aeschylus' most profound and climactic thoughts on this question in the current of action which races violently through the *Agamemnon* and *Choephoroe* to find repose in the lyric note of reconciliation on which the *Eumenides* ends. We must, then, pursue our study of the political motif in the work of Aeschylus with a careful analysis of the development of this theme in the *Seven*. A brief survey of the principal explanations that have been given of the meaning of the play will serve as an appropriate starting point for our own analysis.[1]

The earliest interpretations, emphasizing Eteocles' actions in the first part of the drama, viewed the play as the story of an "ideal ruler and defender of his city" who voluntarily sacrificed his life for the sake of his country. This interpretation foundered when Eteocles' behavior in the second half of the play was interpreted by critics as running strongly counter to any conception of an ideal ruler. Critics then saw the drama as

1. This survey of interpretations is summarized from the recent study by K. von Fritz, *Antike und moderne Tragödie* (Berlin, 1962), pp. 193–226. See especially pp. 199–200.

falling into two contradictory halves and Wilamowitz asserted that Aeschylus had constructed the *Seven* from two disparate sources which failed to harmonize.[2] Next, Friedrich Solmsen argued that the disharmonious quality of the play had been consciously imposed upon it by Aeschylus and he suggested that it is the action of the Erinys in the second half of the play that occasions a radical transformation of Eteocles' character.[3] More recently, Wolff and Patzer[4] have attempted to show that Eteocles is a victim of the curse from the beginning of the play on, and that his actions can be understood as showing the effect of the curse working upon him in some kind of mystical co-operation with his own will.[5] Patzer calls the first half of the

---

2. The following passages which illustrate Wilamowitz's position are quoted by H. Lloyd-Jones, "The End of the *Seven against Thebes*," *Classical Quarterly*, N.S. IX (1959), 83, 84. In the first, taken from *Griechische Verskunst* (Berlin, 1921), p. 199, Wilamowitz states, "Septem adversus Thebas bipertita est; coniunxit enim Aeschylus interitum Labdacidarum, rem vere tragicam, cum epica fabula, quae Septem ducum cladem celebrabat, neque defendi possit, si quis Aristoteli et Lessingio confisus actionis unitatem neglexisse crimini ei dederit." In the second, taken from *Sitz. Berl. Akad.*, 1903, pp. 438-39, he says, "Sein ganzes Drama hat zwei ganz disharmonische Grundmotive. Die eine ist die Oidipodie, die delphische exemplificatorische Geschichte von dem Ungehorsam des Laios, dem Fluche des Oidipus, dem Untergange der sündigen Brut. Das hat mit dem Wechselmorde der Brüder sein Ende. Das andere ist die siegreiche Verteidigung Thebens gegen die Argeier, der Untergang der Sieben. . . . Hier ist Eteokles der hochherzige Retter des Vaterlandes, der untadelige Held."

3. See F. Solmsen, "The Erinys in Aischylos' *Septem*," *TAPA*, LXVIII (1937), 200-5.

4. See E. Wolff, "Die Entscheidung des Eteokles in den *Sieben gegen Theben*," *Harvard Studies in Classical Philology*. LXIII (1958), 89-95 and H. Patzer, "Die dramatische Handlung der *Sieben*," *HSCP*, LXIII (1958), 97-119.

5. Similar views are expressed by two other recent critics. A. Lesky, "Eteokles in den *Sieben gegen Theben*," *Wien. Stud.*, LXXIV (1961), 15, says, "was von aussen über ihn verhängt ist, das wird zu seiner persönlichen Schuld, weil er das Notwendige in seinen eigenen Willen hineinnimmt, weil er das, was er tun muss, schliesslich auch zu tun begehrt. Das bis tief in die homerische Epik zurückreichende Problem göttlicher und menschlicher Motivation hat hier eine neue, spezifisch aischyleische Fassung erhalten." B. Otis, "The Unity of the *Seven Against Thebes*," *Greek, Roman, and Byzantine Studies*, III (1960), 167-68, writes, "What differentiates the patriotic Eteocles of lines 1-652

play a "Verblendungshandlung" (an action in which the hero is "blinded" to the true nature of the situation in which he finds himself) of the Sophoclean type and sees the second half as representing the outcome of the curse with the resulting atonement for the sins committed by the House of Labdacus. Thus for Patzer the play develops from a "Verblendungshandlung" to "a magnificent resolution which, although a family is thereby extinguished, nevertheless has, in the end, an immensely liberating effect." [6] Finally, Kurt von Fritz makes a major contribution to our understanding of the meaning of the play by emphasizing a factor that had been neglected by many previous interpreters, the psychologically realistic character of all of Eteocles' actions. In speaking of Eteocles' decision to face his brother at the seventh gate, he says: "There remains for him, to be sure, no free decision in the sense that he can choose or not choose the 'voluntary sacrifice of his life' for his city. However, he is still 'free' in the sense that he cannot act differently from the way he acts, because he is the person he is; and that means in this case, a man who is fully conscious of his responsibility and who cannot bear the disgrace of having avoided it." [7]

Von Fritz's emphasis on the realistic character of Eteocles' actions represents a major advance in the scholarly criticism of the play. The Eteocles who emerges from Von Fritz's interpretation is at least a believable human being who dutifully

---

from the desperate man of the following part is simply his new understanding of his situation, of his true relation to both Erinys and Olympians, which breaks upon him when he discovers who his own opponent will be. He sees and rightly sees in the 'chance' which puts Polynices at the seventh gate the very hand of both gods and Erinys. . . . To resist such evident omens and even such a direct, personal challenge would not be prudence, but cowardice. Given his character as previously set forth, his devotion to the city and his responsibility as its ruler, he cannot do other than die with honor. It is not he who has sought or seeks the *miasma* of fraternal bloodshed: it is the *ara* which dooms his house and with which, he now sees, the gods have fully co-operated. Thebes and its gods no longer depend on his safety: *its* safety, on the contrary, demands his own destruction."

6. Patzer, "Die dramatische Handlung der *Sieben*," p. 115.
7. Von Fritz, *Tragödie*, p. 213.

shoulders all of the responsibilities of his office without regard to his personal safety. Von Fritz, however, offers no textual evidence in support of this conception of Eteocles' character and merely allows his judgment to rest upon fiat.[8] Yet so strongly does he feel the nobility of Eteocles' character that in discussing his angry outburst against the chorus after the parodos he says: "Whoever would accept here the interpretation discussed by Patzer only as a possibility, that this passage indicates a weakness of Eteocles or contains even a hint that he is not really a good ruler, would show, by this, that he has completely misunderstood the play." [9]

While accepting Von Fritz's important insight that psychological realism is the key to understanding Eteocles' character, it is my purpose in this chapter to discuss relevant textual evidence that calls into question Eteocles' alleged nobility as a ruler. On the basis of this evidence an analysis of the meaning of the *Septem* will be offered which differs significantly from the interpretations currently accepted.

The first significant evidence for Eteocles' basic character comes from his interchange with the chorus at lines 182–286. Here Eteocles rebukes the chorus for throwing themselves on the images of the gods for divine protection from the imminent attack that threatens the city. The women respond to his angry criticism that their conduct is subverting the morale of the citizens by explaining that the sounds of war at the gates had driven them, in panic, to the images of the gods for protection. To this, Eteocles replies that they would be better advised to pray that the city's defenses withstand the enemy attack. We recognize in this remark the bitter, cynical realism that regularly marks a soldier's attitude toward war. The chorus answers with a prayer for continued divine

---

8. See his discussion in *ibid.*, p. 222. In a review of Von Fritz's book (*Classical Review*, N.S. XIII [1963], 24–27) D. W. Lucas criticizes his interpretation of Eteocles' character with the remark, ". . . but the real objection here is that Eteocles is assumed to be a hero who sacrifices himself to save his city. Why then does the Chorus speak only of an act performed ἀσεβεῖ διανοίᾳ?"

9. Von Fritz, *Tragödie*, p. 219.

protection which infuriates Eteocles because the women are again reaching a point of hysteria that he knows will be dangerous. He warns them not to disobey him with their desperate appeals to the gods but they reply with a conventional reference to the supreme power of the gods and their ability to assist those in great peril. To his claim that the propitiation of the gods is the business of men, they ask why there should be any resentment toward their prayer since it is the gods who preserve the city. Eteocles significantly replies that he does not begrudge them their worship of the gods but that they must not alarm the citizens. Again we see Eteocles taking careful thought for the military aspects of the situation and demanding that the chorus' behavior conform to military necessity. As the conflict draws closer, the women are, however, unable to restrain their fears and pitifully appeal once more to the gods for protection (251, 253, 255). In the course of the ensuing stichomythia, Eteocles rebukes the chorus for speaking of the miseries of the state while impiously touching the statues of the gods. They excuse themselves on the basis of fear, again, and Eteocles warns them to remain silent as the critical moment of assault approaches. The chorus finally yields to his commands and in praising them for their new attitude, he suggests that they abandon the statues of the gods and, in place of their previous, fearful laments, pray that "the gods be our allies" (266). When Eteocles speaks here of god as a "potential ally" we have another clear example of a soldier's point of view. This attitude is emphasized in his own prayer that follows in which he promises to make due sacrifice to the gods provided they protect the city in battle. He recommends that the chorus pray for this also and then adds the realistic afterthought that no one can escape his fate. Thus Eteocles views god as an ally whose aid is to be secured by entreaty, gifts, and sacrifices; his faith accepts the tenets of the conventional religion when they support the demands of tactical expediency and rejects them when they subvert these demands. Indeed, his is a soldier's *Weltanschauung* in which all considerations are subordinated to the demands of the immediate tactical situation. This essential character of Eteocles' faith is boldly emphasized in his remark to the messenger at line 414 that "Ares will decide the battle's outcome with a throw of the dice." This statement, made, significantly, in a context in which Eteocles is attempting to encourage one of his own soldiers, clearly shows that Eteocles' religion consists basically in a belief in the fortunes of war.

We have further important evidence for his attitude in the long central scene of the play in which the seven pairs of opposing warriors are described. Here the messenger places great emphasis on the arrogant behavior of the Argive chieftains before the gates of Thebes. In their behavior as well as the motifs emblazoned on their shields they show their contempt for the will of the gods. Throughout this description, Eteocles advocates the same kind of conventional morality approved by the chorus. Each time occasion permits he emphasizes the piety and humility of his forces as opposed to the *hybris* of the Argive leaders. Here the precepts of conventional morality appear to give Eteocles a tactical advantage and he accepts their implications with alacrity. The weakness and superficiality, however, of this advocacy of the claims of conventional morality are seen at line 677 ff. Here, after Eteocles has indicated that he intends to fight his brother, the chorus attempts to dissuade him by citing the fearful consequences of fratricide in the view of conventional morality. In a vivid figure they remind him that

ἀνδροῖν δ' ὁμαίμοιν θάνατος ὧδ' αὐτοκτόνος—
οὐκ ἔστι γῆρας τοῦδε τοῦ μιάσματος

(*the death, thus, of two men, related in blood, at each other's hands—of this pollution there is no growing old*).

To the chorus' continued insistence that he avoid this conflict he replies that the present situation has been willed by the gods. This is a recourse to fatalism that is supporting evidence for Eteocles' highly pragmatic faith. He wishes to fight his brother and, indeed, must fight him because, as we shall see, theirs is essentially a struggle for power and the possession of

Thebes. If one aspect of conventional religion opposes his desires as a soldier and ruler then he takes recourse in another aspect which approves anything that happens as the will of the gods. In a similar vein when the chorus presses the issue further, citing the guilt that attaches to slaying someone of related blood, Eteocles appeals to the curse of his father, as we have noted (695–97), as the cause of his actions. This cause, like the reference to the gods' will, must be understood as a rationalization of his intention to fight to maintain his authority and possessions. Again with a soldier's cynicism he cites whatever scripture will justify his actions. To the chorus' suggestion that he pray to the gods to avert the avenging curse, he does not respond with acquiescence in conventional piety as he did when condemning the arrogance of the Argive leaders. Rather, he ignores the chorus' suggestion and replies that the gods have abandoned him and will take pleasure only in his death (702–4). The chorus' insistence that the will of the gods may be changed by prayer brings the response of Eteocles that the raging curse of Oedipus is taking its effect (709). Once more this expression of belief in the power of the curse serves as a convenient means of justifying his intention to fight against his brother. When the chorus asks in unrestrained horror if he really means to shed kindred blood, he replies again, with his infallible ability to pit one doctrine of conventional religion against another, that none may escape the evils the gods have given. This is a facile rationalization for any action one may wish to take and it is consistent with the direction of Eteocles' thought that we have described up to this point. We have seen that Eteocles accepts the tenets of conventional religion when they support personal or tactical advantage, as in regard to the impious boasting of the Argive leaders, and that he rejects them when they oppose such advantage as is shown by his sharp rebuke to the chorus at the beginning of the play for their uncontrolled appeals to the gods. Eteocles' character is clearly expressed by the two articles of faith he actually lives by: that Ares decides the outcome of events with dice (414) and that one strikes a bargain with the gods, as with one's allies, to reward them if they render assistance (266 ff.). Eteocles thus uses conventional religion, as Alexander the Great is said to have used oracles, as the servant, not the master, of his policy. In the description of Eteocles in this play there is no textual evidence to justify the view that he is acting as an ideal ruler. He is described as an efficient, often cynical, soldier who knows that the prime responsibility of a military leader is to subordinate all considerations to the demands of military necessity. All of his actions and thought bear witness to this attitude and all of them are easily and clearly explicable in terms of it. We are able to understand Eteocles' behavior in realistic terms and we need not have any recourse to the theme of the curse on the House of Labdacus which has played such a prominent role in the criticism of this play. We have seen that Eteocles, himself, treats the curse merely as an instrument of military policy and this should be a warning to us to be suspicious of it as a motivating force in the play.

Since the chorus is the other major agent in the play that alludes to the curse we must now discuss the importance of their reference to this theme. The chorus first speaks of the curse during their attempt to dissuade Eteocles from opposing Polynices, where we have noted that they argue strongly against his insistence on the necessity of the curse's fulfillment. The chorus, in rebuttal of Eteocles' appeal to the "will of god," calls upon other aspects of the traditional religion to avert what they know can only be a religious catastrophe, the slaughter of brother by brother. However, after Eteocles' departure from the stage to meet his brother in combat, they break out into a fearful lament in which they recount the history of the curse and conclude with a statement of their fear that the avenging spirit of Oedipus will accomplish his angry oath against his sons. With the struggle between Eteocles and Polynices now imminent, the chorus is ready to believe in the effectiveness of the curse as a terrifying possibility. Then, after the messenger has announced the actual fact of the brothers' death, the chorus fearfully blames the curse of Oedipus for the outcome (832 ff.). They repeat their belief in the efficacy of the curse when addressing Ismene and Antigone who come to learn of their brothers' fate (886–87), and they conclude their conversation with the sisters in this scene on a note of lament emphasizing the victory of the curse (951–55).

To evaluate properly the significance of the chorus' attitude toward the curse, we must remember that it is regularly portrayed in the play as a frightened, ineffective body that yields completely to its emotions. The women exhibit no excess of spiritual or intellectual virtue and they draw their judgments exclusively, if not consistently, from the tenets of the traditional religion. Their fearful outbursts, however, are highly appropriate to their character as essentially weak and helpless human beings. Under these circumstances we cannot be meant to take, as serious and perceptive insights into the inner workings of the plot of the *Seven*, the thoughts of this band of women whose minds are distraught by a near frenzy of fear.

We have seen that the curse as a theme in the play derives its importance principally from references to it made by Eteocles and the chorus. In the case of Eteocles we noted that his basic religious outlook is highly pragmatic and subordinated to his role as a soldier and ruler of Thebes. He is able to manipulate all of the doctrines of the conventional religion to suit his purposes and will. As for the chorus, we saw that the curse is a doctrine of their traditional religious belief which they respect or challenge as their fears drive them. The position, therefore, that the curse on the House of Laius, promulgated as it is by Eteocles and the chorus, is meant to have a significant effect on the course of the plot of the *Seven* is untenable. Yet the statements of Eteocles and the chorus concerning the curse have been accepted on face value by many critics. In reading a passage from *Othello,* however, it would be a matter of essential importance to know if it were spoken by Iago, Desdemona, or Othello. The character of each of these would materially influence our attitude toward what they say. The same principle, I submit, is valid here.[10] Since the use of the curse as an explanatory principle in this play is subject to the criticism made above, we have justification for abandoning it in favor of a realistic interpretation of Eteocles' character which bears fruitful results.

We gain support for this interpretation from the appearance in the play of Antigone and Ismene. Unfortunately the manuscript assignments of lines to the sisters are not secure.[11] Yet from the time they are first mentioned as appearing on stage (862), a clearly defined theory of causation for the events in the play is counterpointed against the theme of the curse on the House of Laius. In Murray's text the lines which manifest this new theory are assigned to Ismene, and I have accepted his arrangement of the text as a logical one. The basic cause of the events which occur in the *Seven* is hinted at once and then expressed quite clearly in the conversation the sisters have with the messenger after he has announced the death of Eteocles and Polynices. At lines 882–85 Ismene says:

ἰὼ ἰὼ δωμάτων
ἐρειψίτοιχοι καὶ πικρὰς μοναρχίας
ἰδόντες, ἤδη διήλ-
λαχθε σὺν σιδάρῳ

(*Alas! Alas! Overthrowers of the walls of your homeland, and gazers upon bitter single rule, now you are reconciled by the sword*).

Here Eteocles and Polynices are not excused by reference to Oedipus' curse but rather they are openly chided as strugglers for power and single rule.[12] This is what Ismene suggests as the

10. The relationship between thought and character is noted by Aristotle, with his accustomed perception, in the *Poetics* 1454a16–1454a36.
11. See the discussion of this problem by Lloyd-Jones, "The End of the *Seven against Thebes*," pp. 104–8.
12. Commentators have remarked on the reference of ἐρειψίτοιχοι to Polynices and πικρὰς μοναρχίας ἰδόντες to Eteocles. On this passage, see A. Sidgwick, *Aeschylus: "Septem contra Thebas"* (Oxford, 1903), p. 59, and T. G. Tucker, *The "Seven Against Thebes" of Aeschylus* (Cambridge, 1908), p. 179.

reason for their downfall in place of the inexorable working out of a curse. Then at lines 902–6 Ismene gives clear voice to what she obviously understands is the real cause of the events that have happened when she says:

$$\mu\acute{\epsilon}\nu\epsilon\iota$$
$$<\delta\grave{\epsilon}>\ \kappa\tau\acute{\epsilon}\alpha\nu'\ \grave{\epsilon}\pi\iota\gamma\acute{o}\nu\text{ois},$$
$$\delta\iota'\ \grave{\omega}\nu\ \alpha\grave{\iota}\nu o\mu\acute{o}\rho o\iota\varsigma,$$
$$\delta\iota'\ \grave{\omega}\nu\ \nu\epsilon\hat{\iota}\kappa o\varsigma\ \check{\epsilon}\beta\alpha$$
$$\kappa\alpha\grave{\iota}\ \theta\alpha\nu\acute{\alpha}\tau o\upsilon\ \tau\acute{\epsilon}\lambda o\varsigma$$

(*For those who come after them the possessions remain, on account of which, on account of which, strife and the consummation of death have overtaken the ill-starred brothers*).

Now, clearly and unequivocally, we are told the cause of the strife and death of the two brothers was their struggle for the possession of Thebes.[13] Here we have an analysis of cause that is Thucydidean in its clarity as it pierces through the romantic, Herodotean web of family pollution, curse, and destruction and sees the contest between the two brothers for what it is—a personal struggle for power and wealth. Thus the aspiration for material possessions and sole rule are the clearly expressed causes of the tragic events of the play. This explanation of the theme of the *Seven* is further supported by events which have occurred earlier in the play. The long central scene of the *Seven* consists of the description of the seven pairs of leaders who will face each other at the gates of the city. Throughout the description of the first six pairs of warriors the emphasis, with one exception, is on the contrast in piety shown by the Argive and Theban chieftains. Eteocles makes much, as we have seen, of the arrogance of his opponents and feels that

---

13. Most commentators and translators have accepted this interpretation of the passage but they have failed to see its significance. Wilamowitz, for example, who strongly emphasized the theme of the curse, translated this passage in *Aischylos: Interpretationen* (Berlin, 1914), pp. 83–84, as follows: "Dieser Besitz, der nicht nur Ursache, sondern Urheber ihres Haderns und Sterbens war . . . bleibt den Nachkommen."

their attitude gives him a moral, and therefore tactical, advantage. The climax toward which this scene is directed is the description of the seventh pair of warriors, Eteocles and Polynices. Here, however, the theme of piety and impiety is superseded by a different and more important one for the plot of the play. Emblazoned on the shield of Polynices, the messenger tells us, is the figure of *Dike* and she is portrayed as saying that she will lead Polynices back to his native city. Eteocles, in a blustering speech, rejects the symbolism of his brother's shield by denying that Polynices had ever in his life served the cause of justice. His outburst, dominated as it is by powerful emotion, offers, however, no proof of his charges. Here in the culminating episode of the first part of the *Seven* the issue clearly turns on who has the right, sanctioned by justice, to rule the city of Thebes.[14] Eteocles and Polynices meet each other in fatal combat to contest this right, thus confirming Ismene's statement that the cause of the struggle was rivalry for material possessions and power.[15] The shield of Polynices and Eteocles' reaction to it clearly tell us that a question of justice, emerging from the clash of rival ambitions, is central to the meaning of the play. Thus we have here as the essential, unified theme of the *Seven* contending assertions of the right to rule which, because no other way is desired or contemplated, are settled by an appeal to force which ends in disaster for the rival claimants. The tragic consequences of the struggle between Eteocles and Polynices indicate that Aes-

---

14. D. Kaufmann-Bühler, *Begriff und Funktion der Dike in den Tragödien des Aischylos* (Bonn, 1955), pp. 50-59, is one of the few critics who has seen the importance of Justice as a theme in the play. He understands Polynices' attack on his native city as a violation of divine law and comments (p. 54), "Trotz der schiefen Lage, in der Eteokles sich vom Standpunkt des menschlichen Rechts aus befindet, hat er mit seiner Verurteilung des Polyneikes vollkommen recht. Denn er meint die göttliche Dike, gegen die Polyneikes sich vergeht." It is argued in this chapter, however, that the real issue in the play concerns the moral failure, exclusively on the human level, to settle a question of conflicting claims of justice.

15. That this is also Polynices' view of the nature of his quarrel with Eteocles is clearly seen from ll. 631-38.

chylus meant to make the strongest possible condemnation of this use of arms to settle a matter of justice. The world which he describes here has not reached that level of moral development that would permit it to substitute another, higher approach to that of force. We know, however, from the *Oresteia* what direction that superior approach was to take.

It is interesting to note that this theme of conflicting claims to justice appears again in the final scenes of the play, whose authenticity has been the subject of spirited controversy.[16] The many complicated factors that relate to the question of the genuineness of this section have been discussed with admirable thoroughness by Lloyd-Jones, and the reader interested in the history and scope of the problem is well advised to turn to his work.[17] What is important to the thesis of this paper is that we have important evidence linking the action of the disputed scenes to the theme that I have argued is basic to the *Seven*. At line 1049 Antigone, who has asserted her intention to bury Polynices, justifies her conduct to the herald by saying that her brother only returned evil for evil he suffered. The herald replies in the next line that Polynices' actions were unjustly directed against the entire state instead of the one guilty party. In this interchange between Antigone and the herald the rival claims of justification of the two brothers at the end of the shield scene are called to mind. Antigone defends Polynices on the basis of his requiting evil for evil; the herald justifies Eteocles' action and the decision not to bury Polynices on the basis that it is unjust to make a whole city suffer for one man.

16. Wilamowitz had arbitrarily declared in *Aischylos: Interpretationen*, p. 88, that "Eigentlich bedarf es über die Unechtheit keiner Worte mehr, und wer sie Bergk (Litt. Gesch. III 302), Corssen (Antigone des Sophokles S. 29) und mir (Sitz. Ber. 1903, 436) nicht geglaubt hat, wird unbelehrbar bleiben, und man kann den Leuten nicht verwehren, daß sie auf ihre Unempfindlichkeit für Stil und Poesie pochen: auch im Drama muss man die Stumpfheit der Einheitshirten gewähren lassen wie im Homer." Lloyd-Jones, in the able study that has frequently been cited in this paper, has shown that the matter is still in dispute.

17. In *ibid.*, Lloyd-Jones discusses all of the relevant aspects of this problem and provides a comprehensive bibliography.

Thus once again an argument about the justification of human actions is raised and inconclusively settled because no means of handling the dispute is available besides force. Antigone's intransigence, we know from the legend, will lead to consequences no less fatal than Eteocles' conflict with Polynices; for the appeal to force achieves only tragic results. This problem is highlighted further by the half-chorus that goes to bury Polynices when it alludes at lines 1070-71 to the relativity of justice in a state that calls different things just at different times. We see, then, that the theme emphasized in the allegedly spurious last scenes of the *Seven* is the same as that of the undisputed part of the drama; for we have here, in this section of the play also, the rivalry of contending claims of justice. If the final scenes are genuine then they indicate that a consistent motif runs throughout the play; if they are spurious then they at least indicate that the skillful forger who added them understood the importance of the theme of justice in the play.[18]

The interpretation of the *Seven* that has been presented above is opposed in significant detail to all other previous, major interpretations of the play. Lloyd-Jones has made a perceptive and thorough analysis of these interpretations and has added one of his own which disputes the conclusions of his predecessors.[19] It is now necessary for me to relate my position to these previous views and to indicate the basis on which it differs from them. The major differences in interpretation of the play are conveniently analyzed by Lloyd-Jones in regard to differences in interpretation of the three key passages in the *Seven* given below.[20]

---

18. That a skillful forgery is possible is indicated by both D. Kaufmann-Bühler, *Begriff und Funktion der Dike in den Tragödien des Aischylos*, p. 58 and Lloyd-Jones, "The End of the *Seven against Thebes*," p. 114.

19. The history of many of the problems connected with the interpretation of the *Seven* is described, lucidly and in detail, by Lloyd-Jones, "The End of the *Seven against Thebes*," pp. 80-115. I am indebted to his article for a number of references to relevant work of other scholars.

20. For purposes of my subsequent analysis I have quoted ll. 902-6 in passage (2). Lloyd-Jones cites only ll. 902-3.

(1) ἢ τοὺς μογεροὺς καὶ δυσδαίμονας
ἀτέκνους κλαύσω πολεμάρχους (827-28)

(*Or shall I bewail the miserable and ill-starred childless generals?*)

(2) μένει
<δὲ> κτέαν' ἐπιγόνοις,
δι' ὧν αἰνομόροις
δι' ὧν νεῖκος ἔβα
καὶ θανάτου τέλος (902-6)

(*For those who come after them the possessions remain, on account of which, on account of which, strife and the consummation of death have overtaken the ill-starred brothers.*)

(3) ἐξέπραξεν, οὐδ' ἀπεῖπεν
πατρόθεν εὐκταία φάτις·
βουλαὶ δ' ἄπιστοι Λαΐου διήρκεσαν.
μέριμνα δ' ἀμφὶ πτόλιν·
θέσφατ' οὐκ ἀμβλύνεται (840-44)

(*The oracle prayed for by a father has achieved its end and has not failed; and the disobedient counsels of Laius have endured. There is cause for anxiety concerning the city. The words of god do not lose their edge.*)

Lloyd-Jones summarizes the differing interpretations which have arisen in regard to these passages in the following way. Wilamowitz argued that these passages showed that Aeschylus had loosely combined two disparate traditions.[21] He claimed that (1) ruled out the possibility of sons for Eteocles and Polynices and thus ruled out any possible reference to a successful expedition of the Epigoni in the next generation. However, he interpreted (2) and (3) to refer to the future destruction of the city at the hands of the Epigoni. He explained this apparently very severe discrepancy by the claim that Aeschylus had carelessly combined two separate traditions with the resulting inconsistency in plot. Next Klotz argued

---

21. See his discussion in *Aischylos: Interpretationen*, p. 82.

that (2) and (3) did not in fact refer to the Epigoni tradition.²²
He urged that the ἐπιγόνοις of (2) should be taken in the
general sense of "later generations" and that (3) referred not
to any future event but to the mutual slaughter of the two
brothers which had just occurred. Klotz then explained
Eteocles' action in the play, as Robert had before him, as a
sacrifice to save the city on the grounds that once the race of
Laius had been destroyed the city would be freed from danger.
Lloyd-Jones points out that this interpretation of Eteocles'
actions was effectively refuted by Solmsen, who shows that
there is no textual evidence for it although "ample opportunity" was available for the indication of this fact. Solmsen
substituted for Klotz's interpretation his own view that although the curse was to take its effect on Eteocles "it was
repugnant to Aischylos' moral and religious feeling that the
curse and the catastrophe should include the city." ²³ Lloyd-Jones objects to this interpretation, echoing Solmsen's own
words, that there is no textual evidence for it although
Aeschylus would have had "ample opportunity" to indicate
this point if he had wished. In regard to the three critical
passages we have been discussing, Lloyd-Jones interprets
Solmsen's argument as accepting (1) as the elimination of the
Epigoni tradition; as ignoring (2) without comment; and as
understanding (3) as a vague indication of future trouble
although not involving the Epigoni, a view which Lloyd-Jones
regards as "unconvincing." Lloyd-Jones then presents his own
interpretation designed to eliminate the difficulties inherent in
all previous views he has discussed. He argues first that it is
possible (he says probable) that the ἐπιγόνοις of (2) refers
specifically to the Epigoni tradition. Then he suggests that the
adjective ἀτέκνους ("childless") of (1) need not mean what it
has generally and naturally been taken to mean. He wishes to
accept the interpretation of Johann Müller who understood it
to mean "Male natos," and then added, "filios tamen uterque
habebat" referring to the tradition that Eteocles was the father

22. See his discussion in *Rh. Mus.*, LXXII (1917–18), 616–26.
23. Solmsen, "The Erinys in Aischylos' *Septem*," p. 207.

of Laodamas and Polynices of Thersander.[24] Lloyd-Jones thus interprets ἀτέκνους to mean "ill begotten" or "unfortunate in one's parents" although he freely admits that he can find no actual instance of the word in this sense. He, then, interprets (1) in a way that does not preclude further reference to the Epigoni tradition and understands (2) and (3) as references to that tradition. Thus he claims to have eliminated the inconsistency which troubled Wilamowitz between the content of (1) and that of (2) and (3). He also feels that he has avoided the necessity of making interpretations unwarranted by the text which he found reprehensible in the work of Klotz and Solmsen. He suggests that the advantage which his interpretation has over theirs is that it now provides a consistent textual basis for references to the Epigoni tradition. This, he suggests, would satisfactorily explain why the city, which is threatened by the curse on the House of Laius, is saved here; it is to fall eventual victim to the Epigoni. Lloyd-Jones's views are, however, subject to serious criticism. His interpretation of ἐπιγόνοις in (2), no matter how possible or probable it is, does not eliminate the equally strong possibility that it has the general meaning Klotz suggested of "those born after." Furthermore his interpretation of ἀτέκνους in (1) is as strained and unnatural as the interpretations he has criticized in Klotz and Solmsen. We can sympathize with Lloyd-Jones's contention that if we took this word in a sense other than "childless" it would remove a number of difficulties with which we are faced but that consideration is certainly no license to alter the natural meanings of words.[25]

Thus we find a common difficulty in all of the above

24. Lloyd-Jones, "The End of the *Seven against Thebes*," p. 90, indicates that the basis of Müller's interpretation is the fact that, "ΣM ad loc. offers two explanations of ἀτέκνους; the second is the usual one, but the first is ἐπὶ κακῷ τεχθέντας ."

25. Prof. Lloyd-Jones has kindly informed me *per litt.* that he has revised his view on this point and now accepts the more usual interpretation of ἀτέκνους while still maintaining his position that no one has yet proved that the end of the play is an interpolation. He will deal with these points, in greater detail, in his own forthcoming book on Aeschylus and the reader is advised to see his discussion there.

interpretations. They all either make assumptions that are unwarranted by the text or present an interpretation of textual material that is highly strained and unnatural. The interpretation of the *Seven* that I have argued is based in all particulars on textual evidence. In regard to the three critical passages that have been discussed, I accept the obvious and natural meaning of ἀτέκνους ("childless") in (1) and consequently I accept Wilamowitz' position that all further reference to the Epigoni is precluded; I accept Klotz's view that ἐπιγόνοις in (2) does not refer to the Epigoni but simply to "those born after"; and in regard to (3) I accept again Klotz's interpretation that it refers to the present difficulties of the state, not future ones. However, I do not accept Klotz's hypothesis, unsupported by textual evidence, that Eteocles sacrifices himself so that the city may be saved nor do I accept Solmsen's interpretation, equally unsupported by textual evidence, that Aeschylus had decided that the city should not be involved in the fate of the House of Laius. In place of these hypotheses, I argue that the cause of Eteocles' struggle with Polynices is clearly stated by Ismene at lines 904–6 in passage (2). Here we are told that the two brothers fought to their deaths for material possessions. This theme of a struggle for the possession of the city is developed further by a number of ironic references to the grave as the brothers' meager share in the wealth they sought with their lives.[26] The fact that the city is saved has no theological significance but is simply part of the epic legend, while the mutual slaughter of the two brothers is not the working out of Oedipus' curse but rather the moral that Aeschylus wishes to draw from the story. For in the *Seven* we have a struggle for power and wealth in which no reference is made by the contestants to any other value than their own self-interest. Out of the egoism and impulse toward power that selfishly ignores claims and motivations higher than those of the individual, there comes, Aeschylus tells us in this play, only slaughter, destruction, and misery.

What has been portrayed in the *Seven* has been a contest for

26. See for example ll. 907–8, 911–14, 944–46 and 947–50.

power that is fought out within the limited horizons of self-interest. Here no means are sought to transcend conflicting individual aspirations in order to attain a comprehensive system of justice which would assure the security of the individual and the state. Thus the trilogy of which the *Seven against Thebes* is the last play ends on the moral plane on which the *Oresteia* begins.[27] In the *Oresteia* individual claims of self-justification are linked in a chain of continuing retribution which is not broken until an appeal is made in the *Eumenides* to an institution that is superior to these individual assertions of right. The establishment of the Council of the Areopagus in the *Oresteia* symbolizes the triumph of this institution, the rule of law based on reason, as the authoritative force in human society. In the *Seven* Aeschylus has portrayed the tragic consequences that result in a society that has not yet attained the moral level of the *Eumenides*.

Athena and Apollo and the virtues associated with them—reason, wisdom, and enlightenment—emerge victorious in the *Oresteia* as that trilogy ends with a hymn of praise for a new, beneficent world order based on the rule of law.[28] These gods and the virtues they symbolize are, however, totally absent from the *Seven*. In their place are the anger, strife, discord, and violence which lead inexorably to death and destruction; and this should not surprise us for we have long known that the *Seven against Thebes* is a "drama bristling with Ares."[29]

---

27. Others have seen, for different reasons, that the *Seven* represents a stage of moral development that is prior to that of the *Oresteia*. See J. H. Finley, Jr., *Pindar and Aeschylus* (Cambridge, Mass., 1955), pp. 244–45 and Solmsen, "The Erinys in Aischylos' *Septem*," pp. 207–9.
28. See ll. 976–87 of the *Eumenides* for an eloquent statement of the difference in mood between the works under discussion.
29. The well-known phrase of Aristophanes occurs in the *Frogs* at l. 1020. Some commentators have placed exceptional emphasis on the literal references to war in this play. See G. Murray, *Aeschylus: The Creator of Tragedy* (Oxford, 1940), pp. 134–35, 141–43 and T. G. Rosenmeyer, *The Masks of Tragedy: Essays on Six Greek Dramas* (Austin, 1963), pp. 5–48. Military imagery plays, of course, a prominent role but the major issue remains a moral one. The physical warfare that surrounds Thebes symbolizes the moral failure that is central to the theme of this drama.

CHAPTER FOUR

POLITICAL DRAMA II

1.

THE CLIMACTIC WORK OF AESCHYLUS' ART, THE *Oresteia*, IS OF central importance for the study of any aspect of the poet's achievement. For the purpose of the present study, which is directed toward clarifying the central themes of Aeschylus' world view, patriotic, political, and religious, the evidence from the *Oresteia* is crucial. We shall discuss the political motif first, because it is the one found in the foreground of the trilogy and because it connects directly with the theme of the *Seven against Thebes*. In the next chapter we will consider the deeply significant theological message of the trilogy. Since the patriotic theme plays a subordinate role in the *Oresteia*, we shall mention it only, in passing, at appropriate places in this chapter.[1]

---

1. The patriotic theme, dominant in the *Persians* and subordinate in several other plays, is a significant part of Aeschylus' world view but it does not rank as of equal importance with the social and religious themes. The special importance of these latter two motifs can be seen from the central position they occupy in the plays that climax Aeschylus' achievement as a poet, the *Oresteia* and the *Prometheus Bound*.

Broadly speaking, the field of imaginative literature is divided into basically symbolic or basically realistic realms. The symbolic poet, like Dante or Milton, directs his art toward illustrating a specific pattern of external reality that derives from his philosophical or religious world view. The essentially realistic poet, like Homer and Shakespeare, directs his primary attention to illuminating basic and profound human experiences and in his work any philosophical or religious considerations must be derived by implication rather than observed from direct statement. Some major poets have occasionally been able to combine, effectively, both symbolic and realistic elements in one work and Aeschylus must be counted among this number. We have argued that Aeschylus was, fundamentally, a symbolic poet but we have also seen in our discussion of Eteocles that at one point in his development he began to combine more realistic representation of character with his ultimate symbolic purposes. This process of uniting realistic characterization and symbolic meaning reaches its brilliant climax in the *Agamemnon*. That the ultimate and transcendent purpose of the *Oresteia* is symbolic is proved beyond question by its terminal play, the *Eumenides;* yet it is in the realism of the *Agamemnon* that we must seek the matrix of the symbolic message borne by the *Eumenides*. The skillful unification of realistic and symbolic themes in this trilogy represents an achievement of the highest order not only for Greek tragedy but for Western literature in general. In analyzing the *Oresteia*, therefore, we must make it a cardinal point of our criticism that the realistic action of the *Agamemnon* is to be understood as the first step in a unified development of thought and action which culminates in the symbolic meaning of the *Eumenides*.

From its beginning to its end the focal point of the action of the *Agamemnon* is Clytemnestra, and our understanding of the play depends directly on our understanding of her character.[2]

---

2. The importance of Clytemnestra's male characteristics in motivating her actions in this play first received its proper emphasis, to my knowledge, in an article by R. P. Winnington-Ingram, "Clytemnestra and the Vote of Athena," *Journal of Hellenic Studies,* LXVIII (1948),

We must now make a detailed analysis of her role in the play and show its relation to subsequent developments in the trilogy. Our attitude toward Clytemnestra is influenced by a number of critical passages, some containing overt, but most containing indirect, yet quite clear, hints about her character. The first of these important passages occurs before a dozen lines of the prologue have been spoken by the guard who in

---

130–47. Winnington-Ingram's interpretation, which came to my attention after this chapter was written, and my own are in agreement concerning the basic characterization and motivation of Clytemnestra although in the citation and interpretation of evidence we differ at various places. We also have a very different view of how the Clytemnestra theme fits into the plan of the entire trilogy. For a very different interpretation of the role of Clytemnestra in this play see H. Lloyd-Jones, "The Guilt of Agamemnon," *CQ*, XII (1962), 187–98 and especially pp. 197, 199. Some scholars have taken the position, disputed in this chapter, that Clytemnestra's actions are at least partially justified. See, for example, J. Jones, *On Aristotle and Greek Tragedy* (New York, 1962), pp. 74–75, 115. H. W. Smyth, *Aeschylean Tragedy* (Berkeley, 1924), pp. 167–73, gives a telling description of Clytemnestra's cruelty and viciousness (p. 172) but nevertheless feels that the reasons she gives in support of her deed are legitimate. We have attempted to show in this chapter that Clytemnestra is a complete and resourceful hypocrite who invents excuses as she needs them and that important justification for this view is to be found in the final two acts of the trilogy. We find strong support for our view in the analysis of A. Sidgwick, *Aeschylus: Agamemnon* (Oxford, 1925), p. xiv, who writes:

The character of Klytaemnestra is given with a masterly force and effect in every stroke. There are no fine shades about the drawing, as there are none in the conception. She is the impersonation of the tyrannic self-will, wronged and angered, and turned to vengeance. She is Homer's οὐλομένη ἄλοχος "an accursed wife:" pitiless, and contemptuous, and unimpassioned, but resolutely bent on revenge, and concentrating her whole Titanic force upon it without misgiving. There is no womanly passion in her, and no trace of weakness. The murder she is bent on is in revenge for her slain child, but we hear scarcely a word of love for Iphigeneia from her lips: the lovely description of the maiden in her father's halls is from the mouth of the chorus; but the mother scarcely mentions her save in the climax of her bitter triumph, when with dreadful irony she pictures her welcoming her sire in Hades (1555). She is an adulteress, but there is no love for her paramour; her unfaithfulness is merely a form of her vengeance: hatred of her husband is the motive of it, not love of Aegisthos. She is crafty, but hers is the craft of a strong and not a weak nature: it is only the needful means to carry out her purpose completely, and the moment the need is over, the mask is scornfully flung aside.

describing his long and weary service introduces an indirect and uneasy note of suspicion toward Clytemnestra. This suspicion commences with his remark that his difficult watch has been commanded by the "male-counselling, hopeful heart of a woman" (10–11). The suggestion that Clytemnestra is playing a role in the state that is not suited to her sex is quietly suggested here although we will not be able to assess its full significance until our analysis proceeds much further. The addition of the adjective "hopeful" may also be taken in a negative sense as a criticism or questioning of the validity of Clytemnestra's commands. That a woman is playing a man's role is a suggestion that something is wrong at Argos and our suspicions are increased when the guard mentions the oppressive fear (14–15) that prevents his falling asleep. He does not specify the source of his fear at this moment but the note of male purposiveness in Clytemnestra's character that has just been sounded can easily be brought into causal connection with the soldier's terror. Further information on the source of the guard's anxiety is found in the explicit statement that he bemoans the royal house "no longer administered in the best way as previously" (18–19). Brought now to the real point of his anguish the guard at the end of his speech suggests with great poetic intensity—although still in a guarded manner—the evil which has descended upon the state. Fervently he prays at line 34 that he may hold his master's hand in his but he desists from going further—a path filled evidently with personal danger—and contents himself with an image, pregnant with threatening significance, that is all he dare say at this moment: "For the rest I remain silent. An ox stands huge upon my tongue[3] and the house if it could speak might do so most clearly. Thus willingly I address those who understand but for those who do not I have forgotten everything" (34–39).

Here the sense of fear and threat are powerfully expressed by the imagery and indirectness of the messenger's speech. Unable

---

3. Richmond Lattimore renders the phrase in this way, capturing the exact nuance of the Greek, in *Aeschylus: Oresteia* in *The Complete Greek Tragedies* (Chicago, 1953), p. 36.

and unwilling to speak openly, the guard casts a deepening suspicion on the current ruler of Argos. We have already heard of Clytemnestra's male nerve when we learned of the soldier's terror in carrying out her orders. Before the first forty lines of the play are spoken we know that a deep-seated evil has infested the state and though no specific charges have yet been lodged we know that this evil is connected with the role that Clytemnestra has been playing in the state in the absence of Agamemnon.

With the appearance of Clytemnestra after the choral ode another quite indirect example of the fear in which she is held is suggested. The chorus says that it would gladly know why Clytemnestra is so joyously conducting sacrifices but quickly adds that there will be no enmity toward her if she keeps silent. Clytemnestra is evidently a person who is known to have a powerful will of her own which is not subject to influence by the wishes of others. The deferential and fearful approach of the chorus is an additional suggestion that an unhealthy situation now exists in the state. Of great interest and importance here is the chorus' reference to the fact that Clytemnestra is now filling the throne of her absent husband (260). The word they use to refer to Agamemnon is ἄρσενος ("male") instead of the appropriate form of ἀνήρ ("husband"). By using this generic term for the male sex the chorus subtly but perceptibly reinforces our association of Clytemnestra with a drive to play a male rather than female role in the state, a theme which began with the guard's characterization of her as "man-counselling."

An angry impatience associated far more with a despotic male nature than a normal woman's is seen in Clytemnestra's exchange with the chorus after the first choral ode. To their hesitance to accept her news of the fall of Troy she responds, with an undercurrent of anger, that she does not take her thoughts from a sleeping mind and with scornful contempt for the chorus' implication that she has the character of a young girl ready to believe any foolish story (275, 277). It is Clytemnestra's mood that is suspect here. The arrogant and bitter tone of "sleepy" (βριζούσης φρενός) and "child" (παιδὸς νέας) shows a spirit accustomed to use scorn and sarcasm to make its point and to rule the will of others.

As proof of her assertion that the Greek army has taken Troy Clytemnestra describes the message system that she has arranged by which flaming beacons have borne the signal of victory, stage by stage, from Troy to Argos. Here she traces with suspicious care the detailed movement of the fiery message as if she felt some special thrill and excitement in recounting the manner by which the news of Agamemnon's triumph reached her. In this intense description of the beacon flames we find lacking a normal woman's concern for a husband absent ten years on a difficult and dangerous military assignment. This uneasy note joins with other warnings we have already received to prepare us for the developments that lead to the criminal act that climaxes the play.

Clytemnestra follows this description with an even more significant passage in which she describes—or rather imagines—the final scene of victory at Troy. Here events and situations that are normally far from the interest and experience of women are described in unnerving detail and with a certain fierce pleasure. The brutal scene of the wives and children of the conquered soldiers falling upon the dead bodies of husbands and fathers is conjured up with intense interest by Clytemnestra (320–29). We would expect most normal women, mindful of their own roles as wives and mothers, to shrink back in horror from such violent thoughts and even the wife of a victorious general might, as a woman, be expected to sympathize with the women and children of the conquered. Then we must notice the excitement and the interest in military detail that Clytemnestra shows when she goes on to describe the activities of the Greek victors. She evokes from her imagination a picture, striking in its realism, of the logistical operations of the Greek army on the night of victory. With an interest, familiarity, and accuracy that belong not to a woman but to a professional soldier she visualizes a scene of victory when the hardships of nightly bivouacs under the open sky can finally be exchanged for victor's rights in the houses of the conquered (330-36). Clytemnestra adds a final disturbing touch to her description when she gratuitously prays that the army commit no impious deed of defilement in Troy (336-41). This may indeed be a danger but it is a strange thought to cross the mind of a normal wife at a moment of conventional joy and happiness. Another uneasy and discordant note has been sounded in our developing analysis of Clytemnestra's character.

Our suspicions of Clytemnestra are further deepened by the conversation of the chorus and Agamemnon's herald at lines 545-50. Here the chorus must maintain a cryptic tone out of obvious fear of Clytemnestra but their statement that the country missed the army as much as the army yearned for the country, that silence was the people's only cure for harm, and that, with Agamemnon gone, there were those they feared so much in the state that death would have been welcome tell us much of the evil that has overtaken Argos at the hands of Clytemnestra. Of the harm that she has worked we can have no better witness than the chorus' statement that death would have been a welcome grace (550). Important aspects of Clytemnestra's character and personality which have been noticed before are emphasized at 11. 587 ff. where, using characteristic sarcasm and scorn, she sharply reminds the chorus of its skepticism and her accuracy when she accepted the evidence of the flaming torches for the fall of Troy. Then the darkest side of Clytemnestra's psyche breaks forth in the feverish, unnatural defense of her virtue which she makes at 1. 600 ff. Here she speaks of her loyalty, fidelity, and honesty with a fulsome intensity that cries out its own hypocrisy. Genuine virtue neither needs nor utilizes such a loud and boastful self-advocacy. The chorus, stirred and perhaps angered by Clytemnestra's outrageous lies, more boldly, yet still with protective irony, remarks on her "clear" speech to the herald of Agamemnon's army (615-16). The chorus fears to give explicit voice to what it knows of Clytemnestra but it cannot and will not restrain itself from combating her with the characteristic weapon of all who are downtrodden and oppressed—irony.

The chorus carries on its undercover struggle with Clytemnestra when Agamemnon appears on the scene. In the last words of their speech of welcome to Agamemnon they speak of those who have lived justly and those who have lived unjustly in the city (807–9). The reference to the latter is undoubtedly a clear yet guarded accusation of Clytemnestra.

Clytemnestra's welcome to Agamemnon advances materially the theme we have developed of her character and personality. She begins with a declaration of her love for her husband (855–57) which would be unnecessary if the real emotion were felt and which can only represent a desperate attempt on her part to hide the truth from him until she can carry out her lethal plot. She has the audacity to speak of the loneliness of a woman when her husband is absent at war although we well know that she had found an effective way to ease her loneliness. Significantly, she uses the word ἄρσενος ("male") to refer to her husband and the use of this generic term again reminds us of the male-female theme that has already appeared several times and will significantly continue to appear throughout the play. This theme reminds us that Clytemnestra is involved in a persistent struggle to reverse the normal male-female relationship by seizing initiative and power from her husband and enforcing her will upon him and the state. Her vivid recounting of the wounds she dreamed Agamemnon sustained is like her view of conquered Troy, a morbidly inappropriate theme in a normal wife's thoughts. The pleasure she gets in lingering over the vision of her husband's body pierced through like a net by the enemy's missiles can only be the product of a warped mind. The hysterical lie she tells of being driven by many false reports of Agamemnon's death to attempt often to hang herself strikes the same false note as her other excessively vivid imaginings. She arrogantly continues to overstrain her palpable hypocrisies and lies with a description of the uneasy, sleepless nights caused by anxiety for her husband (891–94). The speech culminates with praise of Agamemnon so false and contrived as to advertise its insincerity in every word. Greeting a husband ten years absent Clytemnestra finds time to describe him as the "watchdog of the house, saving forestay of a ship, firm pillar of a high roof, only child of a father, land appearing to sailors beyond their hope and a flowing spring for a thirsty traveler" (896–901). All of this description, so overwrought, intricate, and artificial, is damning evidence of Clytemnestra's desperate hypocrisy.

Her speech of welcome reaches its climax with the invitation to Agamemnon to walk upon the purple carpet. Her husband's reaction to this speech is highly significant. At line 914 ff. he recognizes that there is something deeply wrong with Clytemnestra's welcome. It was, he notes, much too long and even more significant it is accompanied, in Agamemnon's own words, by an attempt to make a woman out of him (καὶ τἆλλα μὴ γυναικὸς ἐν τρόποις ἐμὲ ἄβρυνε) and to force him to violate the respect owed the gods. Clytemnestra's endeavor to assume male dominance and to force upon her husband the female role of submission is given clear emphasis here. This theme is intensified in the *agon* between Clytemnestra and Agamemnon which follows this speech. Here Clytemnestra uses all of her skill in her successful attempt to defeat Agamemnon's reluctance to tread upon the purple carpet. Agamemnon senses what is at stake and says significantly in the midst of their discussion, "It is not a woman's part to desire strife" (940). He sees that Clytemnestra is attempting to play the dominant role and thus necessarily force a reversal of his role in the process. Although he knows this he cannot carry through his resolve to fight it because Clytemnestra, with superior power and craft, undercuts his resistance by feigning a submissive weakness in order to conquer his will. Clytemnestra wins this initial battle and the moment of her total victory draws closer.

Clytemnestra's treatment of Cassandra supports the general interpretation of her character that we have been making. She begins with a typically hypocritical display of gentleness

(1035-43) in which she congratulates Cassandra on having found masters whose wealth is long-founded and who are thus more kindly disposed to their slaves than the *nouveaux riches*. This is gratuitous hypocrisy and it contains a gratuitous insult to Cassandra who has fallen from royal estate to servility. The unmotivated and unnecessary ferocity of Clytemnestra in this scene bursts forth from the same dark, subterranean psychic sources that are responsible for the basic drive for male dominance that has characterized her action throughout the play. At this point, as well as previously, this drive has destroyed the customary female capacity for compassion and replaced it with an unnatural violence and cruelty. The brittle veneer of Clytemnestra's hypocritical gentleness is quickly broken at line 1065 where we find her hurling sardonic taunts at Cassandra in the feverish, impassioned way that regularly characterizes her thought and language. Instead of womanly sympathy for one caught in a type of distress that is particularly anguishing for a woman to bear, we hear the male soldier's cry of vengeance and imperious command from her throat. It is the chorus of aged men who alone expresses pity for Cassandra and their response makes a marked and significant contrast to Clytemnestra's mood as she leaves the stage.

So far in the play the attack on Clytemnestra has necessarily been kept on the indirect level of innuendo by a chorus that fears to challenge her openly. It is first at l. 1227 ff. that an open denunciation of Clytemnestra is made and this is done by Cassandra who, knowing that she is going to her death, has nothing further to lose. Here Cassandra explicitly charges Clytemnestra with hypocrisy and treachery and says, significantly for our interpretation of her character, "the female is the murderer of the male" (1231). The generic words for male ($ἄρσενος$) and female ($θῆλυς$) appear here and bear additional witness to the theme of Clytemnestra's striving for male dominance that has characterized her action throughout the play. It is with outraged astonishment that Cassandra remarks on the unnatural state of affairs when "the female is the murderer of the male." She goes on to recount other actions that are consistent with our over-all interpretation of Clytemnestra's character. Cassandra describes how Clytemnestra raised a cry of joy "as if in battle" (1236) in her seeming pleasure at Agamemnon's return. With all of this clear denunciation of Clytemnestra, the chorus can still not conceive of a woman as capable of such a deed of violence as the murder of Agamemnon and they ask in somewhat dull perplexity "at the hands of what man" Agamemnon will fall. Here again the unnaturalness of Clytemnestra's role as a woman is emphasized.

With the striking of the actual blows and Agamemnon's shouts of pain, the fierce, male audacity of Clytemnestra reaches its fulfillment. As the crime is carried out the chorus debates what action to take and in the course of its discussion suggests several times what the object of Clytemnestra's plot has been—the seizure of power in the state (1354–55, 1362–63, and 1364–65). Political usurpation is not usually a goal associated with a woman's hopes and aspirations and its attribution here to Clytemnestra emphasizes again her anomalous role in the play.

When Clytemnestra appears on the scene at 1372 ff. she tells us explicitly all we need to know to corroborate all of the more indirect evidence that we have discussed. Now that Agamemnon is dead, she acknowledges her hypocrisy in an open and shameless way. Worse yet is her description of the deed she has just accomplished. She recounts in gory detail how she threw a net, as if for fish, over her husband, "an evil wealth of garment" she calls it. Then she relives with feverish intensity the blows and the groans that brought Agamemnon to his knees and then the final, invincible blow that was driven home she says as a "votive offering" to Zeus, savior of the dead below. The cruelty of the next lines is unbelievable and, as we quote them in full, we see in the clearest form yet the sick and violent hate of a mind driven askew by a powerful, demonic desire to rule, to play the male role, to be the lord and master: "And so, having fallen, he gasps up his life and, breathing out the sharp butchery of his blood, he strikes me with a dark shower of gory dew and I rejoice no less in it than the grain in the field rejoices in heaven-sent rain at the time of the bursting of its bud" (1388-92).

We see here a pathological excitement that deepens our suspicion of Clytemnestra's character and motives. Her almost sensual pleasure in recounting the blows she struck and the feeling of ecstatic joy which she shows when describing the shower of blood from Agamemnon's body, together with the incredible comparison that she makes of rejoicing in this blood as much as a rich crop rejoices in rain, tell us without doubt that we are dealing here with a tormented spirit that has been driven beyond the pale of normal human behavior.

In the scene of remonstrance which follows, the chorus warns Clytemnestra of punishment to come for her horrible crime. Challenged openly now by the chorus on the basis of her own arrogant admissions, Clytemnestra begins a passionate series of rationalizations and attempted justifications of herself that are marked by intense desperation. Now for the first time she mentions the "guilt" of Agamemnon in slaying Iphigeneia, hoping to allay the chorus' wrath by suggesting the principle that "evil begets evil." To this she adds one of her characteristic threats that if the chorus intends to accuse her, it had better have sufficient force to back up its accusations or she will teach it to be temperate in old age (1423-25). Again we see Clytemnestra playing the male role of ruler and conquerer trying to force the chorus into a submissive and secondary position. The chorus, undaunted, repeats its warning that she must pay for her crime and she again passionately attempts to defend her action by attacking Agamemnon's guilt in taking Cassandra as his mistress. Alleging the taking of a mistress as justification for the brutal murder and even more brutal pleasure which she has derived from it is clearly a wild, rationalizing shot in the dark by Clytemnestra who is being pressed harder and harder by the chorus' outraged cries for vengeance. In its response to these remarks the chorus emphasizes again that Agamemnon died "at the hands of a woman" (1453), suggesting once more the theme of Clytemnestra's "male" role in this play. This emphasis is intensified by the fact that the phrase "at a woman's hand" is repeated twice here (1453–54). The thought of a destructive female brings to the chorus' mind the name of Helen whom they charge as an additional possible cause of the evil that has beset them. Clytemnestra feels a curious sympathy for Helen, perhaps a common bond with another woman whose actions caused much harm, and she urges the chorus not to blame her (1462–67). In a now confused seeking for the real cause of the terrible evil that has occurred the chorus mentions the *daimon* of the House of Tantalus which works its power through women and Clytemnestra eagerly grasps at this "causation" as the "true" one (1468–74). Clytemnestra like Eteocles in the *Septem* shows an eagerness to accept a "curse" as the cause of events and the reason is not difficult to understand. Under the aegis of a "curse" any human action can be justified since one may simply cite oneself as the innocent and inevitable victim of transcendent forces. The cynical and evil and guilty have always put their faith in a "curse" or "fate" or some other such inexorable force which relieves them from any personal moral responsibility for their actions. Indeed, such individuals, caught red-handed as Clytemnestra is here, have no alternative defense open to them. It is in the light of attempting to relieve themselves of personal moral responsibility for their actions that we must see both Clytemnestra's acceptance of the "curse" as a causative principle in this play (1475–80) and Eteocles' references to such a force in the *Septem*. So blatant has Clytemnestra's crime been that the shocked chorus easily sees through her hypocritical refuge in the "curse" and in an outraged response asks how anyone could call her innocent in Agamemnon's death (1505–06). Even the chorus which shows rather average intellectual and moral capabilities will not be bullied by Clytemnestra into accepting a "curse" as the responsible agent in Agamemnon's death. The furthest that they will go will be to attribute a helping hand to such a curse (1507–8) but they assert that Clytemnestra cannot claim exoneration from guilt on this basis.

Failing to mollify the chorus with her wild invocation of the familial curse, Clytemnestra desperately returns to the theme of Iphigeneia's death. To cite maternal love as the cause of a husband's murder seems somewhat arrogant for a mother who had sold her son into slavery.[4] Moreover, the action of the *Choephoroe* indicates that Clytemnestra was not able to convince her two children that protective affection for them necessitated Agamemnon's death. Electra and Orestes are not taken in by Clytemnestra's wild rationalizations; neither should we be. The true cause of Clytemnestra's murder of her husband will have to explain the mad and vicious pleasure which she takes in killing the father of her children and the undying hatred of those children for her. The twisted character of Clytemnestra is pointed up by the nature of the thoughts which come into her mind as she carries on her argument with the chorus. When the chorus asks who will bury Agamemnon, angrily discounting her right to do this, she asserts that she has every intention of performing this act and conjures up, with the same suspicious intensity we noted in her visions of the scene of conquered Troy, the picture of Iphigeneia welcoming her father as he descends to Hades (1555-59). The sarcasm and passion of this scene further intensify our feelings of uneasiness concerning Clytemnestra's alleged justifications for her act. Here we have another example of the frenzied state of mind which has regularly characterized her utterances and which, in our view, can be traced to the deep psychic drives which have led Clytemnestra to attempt to overcome her subordinate female role and to strive to replace her husband as the dominant figure in the state. The chorus is now confused by all of the evil it has seen and again speaks of the familial curse on the House of Atreus. Nothing is more pleasant for Clytemnestra to hear as she seeks to escape the charge of personal guilt. She cries out again that this is the true explanation of the murder of Agamemnon but she adds a thought, out of sheer necessity, which clearly shows the flimsy insincerity of her allusions to the curse as a causative agent. When she says that

4. See *Choephoroe*, 1. 915.

she is willing to make a compact with the evil *daimon* in the hope that it will now depart and haunt another family we have final proof of her arrogant hypocrisy. The curse has been useful to her as a shield to hide behind while carrying out the murder of Agamemnon but now that she has the power in the state it would be highly inconvenient to have a curse hanging over *her* head. She might well fear the angry restiveness of subjects who suspected they were not only being ruled by a vicious and criminal queen (such suspicions, we have seen, were already held) but also by an accursed one. The curse clearly is a matter of policy for Clytemnestra, as it was for Eteocles, to be used when needed as a covering rationalization but to be dropped in the crudest possible fashion when it is no longer convenient.[5]

The appearance of Aegisthus at this point in the play gives further evidence for the themes which we have developed in our analysis so far. In his appearance Aegisthus boasts of the justice of Agamemnon's murder because of the crime of Atreus and takes the deepest pleasure in the act though he did not participate in its physical accomplishment. His personal contribution, he tells us with some pride, was the successful planning of the murder. When the chorus warns that he will be stoned, he threatens the old men with cruel punishment in his cowardly and tyrannical way. In response, the chorus sums

---

5. E. R. Dodds, "Morals and Politics in the *Oresteia*," *Proc. of the Cambridge Philological Society*, N.S. VI (1960), p. 30, accepts actual daemonic influence as a causal factor in Clytemnestra's behavior. This view directly conflicts with the attempt made in this chapter to show that there is a clear psychological explanation of Clytemnestra's actions and the invocation of supernatural forces is neither necessary nor desirable. Dodds's general comment, cited in Chapter I, that it was Aeschylus' purpose to lead man out of the daemonic world into a higher one governed by reason is consistent with the attempt made in this chapter to find a motivation, understandable in rational terms, for Clytemnestra's behavior. The basic thesis of the interpretation presented in this chapter is certainly in harmony with Dodds's statement in the article cited in this footnote (p. 31, n. 4) that, ". . . it should be unnecessary to add that underneath its time-bound purpose and its archaic presuppositions the *Oresteia* is also an enduring symbol of certain moral tests and torments which will always be part of the human condition."

POLITICAL DRAMA II   [77]

up its opinion of Aegisthus in one significant insult γύναι "woman" (1625-27). Aegisthus is a "woman" because in cowardly fashion he has stayed away from war, defiling Agamemnon's bed and plotting Agamemnon's death in a most treacherous and unmasculine manner. But he is a "woman" in a far more significant way for this study in that he has taken up the submissive and secondary role that is customary for a woman in political life but which Clytemnestra was unwilling to accept and which appears to have been the psychological source of her acts of violence. Having found Aegisthus, a man willing to play a woman's role, Clytemnestra now has an appropriate mate in place of Agamemnon, a man who vigorously insisted on playing a man's role.

The weakness of Aegisthus is seen in all of his snarling threats hurled at the chorus. These old men who fearlessly challenge him are treated with bitter abuse and dire threats of physical torment. Only a frightened coward could react in this way and this is essentially Aegisthus' character. The chorus continues to ridicule his weakness and subordination to Clytemnestra, his "female" role (1633-35), to which he unconvincingly protests that this has been a tactical necessity and, then, stung by their bitter and valid criticism he rages against the chorus with more threats of physical violence. The chorus again playing upon the transposed male and female roles asks (1643) why he, the man, did not kill Agamemnon instead of allowing the victim's wife to do it and bring pollution on the land. To this question no answer is given but Aegisthus summons the guard to inflict physical punishment on the chorus (1649-51). Before that point is reached, however, Clytemnestra assumes the male role she has fought so hard to win and halts Aegisthus' plans and his guards (1654 ff.). Her mood here is very different from her previous appearances in the play. Earlier she had been characterized by a fierce passion, vivid imagination, and a full capacity for scorn, sarcasm, and hypocrisy. In addition, previously, she had shown all of the intensity and male strength of purpose that was needed to carry out a brutal murder and to defend herself against any outcry for punishment or vengeance. Now that her purpose is accomplished, now that the object of her hatred is dead, Clytemnestra's defiant spirit and intensity of purpose subside and we find her here in the ebb tide of her passion, worn out by her struggle. The Clytemnestra whom we now see neither threatens nor warns, uses neither sarcasm nor scorn, but rather calmly and wearily tells the chorus to go home, speaks in favor of accepting the present situation as it is, and sees herself and the state as being "struck by the heavy hoof of the daemon" (1657-60). Clytemnestra's fierce temper, which had exploded into brutal murder, now that her terrible goal has been accomplished, dies down to a flickering ember of wrath.

The weak and cowardly Aegisthus, hurt by the taunts of the chorus, still sputters his outrage looking for some form of vengeance (1662-64). The chorus in total contempt of him continues its tirade of insults to which he can only mutter ineffectual threats of future punishment. Here we see Aegisthus as a weak and secondary figure who is just the person to play the submissive and dependent role that Clytemnestra demands of her male consort. As Clytemnestra leaves the stage with him at the end of the play she cuts off his angry ranting with the significant remark that "we two ruling will put affairs in order" (1673). "We two ruling" is the keynote of Clytemnestra's life and actions. The achievement of power is the ultimate male goal which she has substituted for normal female aspirations and which has conditioned her to a life of abnormal violence and crime. With Agamemnon out of the way and with Aegisthus dependent upon her she can finally play the role to which she has long aspired.

The first act of the *Oresteia* has, then, been a skillfully worked out and realistically developed "psychological" drama in which we have watched Clytemnestra's drive to attain controlling power in the state achieve a temporary fulfillment. We have argued that this drive to play a dominant, male role in the state is a sufficient and necessary motive for the crime that Clytemnestra commits. Since appropriate data are not given in the play, more subtle psychological speculations as to why

Clytemnestra desires to play such a role must be left unanswered as lying outside of the poet's intention and, consequently, outside of the critic's province.

As we indicated at the beginning of this chapter, the later acts of this trilogy develop the psychological realism of the *Agamemnon* into a theme of far broader and much more symbolic implications. Our task now will be to trace the development of the action begun in the *Agamemnon* through the two plays which succeed it and then to analyze the overlying unity that binds the three stages of the trilogy together.

2.

The leitmotiv of the *Agamemnon* was crime; the leading theme of the *Choephoroe* is vengeance. This theme of vengeance, representing, as it does, the primitive society's response to crime that necessarily unleashes a destructive, self-defeating chain reaction of violence in response to violence, is the binding force between the initial and final stages of the trilogy. For the *Eumenides* will provide a solution, worthy of a highly civilized community, for the problems of crime and punishment that are presented with all of their corrosive influences on society in the first two plays of the trilogy. The *Choephoroe* makes two major contributions to the development of the central theme of the *Oresteia* which it is now our concern to discuss in detail. Its first purpose is to set forth, grimly, the serious limitations of vengeance as an effective response by society to a criminal act; secondly, but also of great significance, it provides numerous indications of the emphatic character of Clytemnestra's guilt as these serve as background and justification for Electra and Orestes' thirst for vengeance. Let us now examine the evidence for these dominant motifs.

Early in the play at ll. 18–19 Orestes calls on Zeus to permit him to take vengeance for the murder of his father. The choral ode which follows Orestes' vow of punishment against his father's murderers describes the mood of sullen, restive obedience the citizens have yielded their rulers since Agamemnon's death. When the chorus says, "But success, this is a god and even more than a god amongst mortals," (59–60) it clearly identifies the "religion" of Clytemnestra and Aegisthus. This has been their only guiding principle and the chorus waits anxiously for a reversal of fortune that will restore the moral order.

Electra then appears on the scene and immediately shows her embarrassed reluctance to bear the libations of her murderess mother to her father's grave. In her invitation to the chorus to advise her on the proper action at this point (100–1) she significantly refers to the common enmity they share toward Clytemnestra and her consort. Electra's consultation of the chorus appears in marked contrast to the highhanded and tyrannical scorn of the general populace that characterizes the behavior of Clytemnestra and Aegisthus. Electra's procedure in seeking advice is treated affirmatively here as is a similar situation in the *Suppliants* where Pelasgus refuses to act without first consulting his people. We may possibly detect here praise for the institutions of democracy as opposed to those of tyranny and see, in this, a subtle expression of the patriotic theme that runs through the work of Aeschylus.

The play's principal theme of vengeance is clearly indicated by the chorus' instruction to Electra to pray that someone will come "who will kill in turn" (121–23). When Electra asks if it is proper to pray for this from the gods the chorus responds by asking how it could not be pious to punish an enemy for evil. Here we clearly see the ethic which dominates the play is one of strict mechanical justice, evil for evil, violence for violence.

Electra then details the crimes she and Orestes have suffered at the hands of a viciously guilty Clytemnestra (124–51). Here again is the play's basic theme of vengeance which demands that blood be paid for blood.

The scene which runs from 164–211 gives us an indication of an important difference of mood between this play and the *Agamemnon*. In the *Choephoroe* the perceptive psychological realism of the *Agamemnon* is replaced by a strangely contrasting artificiality of action in which a lock of hair and footprints are used to establish Orestes' identity. This deliberate abandonment of the careful and convincing realism of the *Agamemnon* establishes the character of the *Choephoroe* as a symbolic rather than a realistic play. It warns us to look for a message in the action, not to seek deeply into the psychological motivations of the principal characters as we did in the *Agamemnon*. We have indicated that the ultimate symbolic significance of the *Choephoroe* is concerned with the principle of vengeance—the principle of the need for automatic sacrifice of a life for a life. The symbolization of vengeance is important in the development of the trilogy because the inadequacy of it as a system of justice must be clearly shown in order to justify the ultimate solution to the problem of crime that is presented in the *Eumenides*.

At lines 235–64 we see the hatred of Orestes and Electra for Clytemnestra clearly expressed as well as the suffering they have endured because of her. Clytemnestra's cruelty to her children is again seen in Electra's description of the treatment she has received from her mother at 11. 444–47.

The chorus' bitterness toward Clytemnestra and Aegisthus is clearly stated at 11. 267–68 where they express the hope of seeing the two murderous conspirators dying in the "pitchy ooze of flame." Electra, Orestes, and the chorus have no doubt whatsoever of the black guilt of Clytemnestra and Aegisthus.

At lines 269 ff. Orestes gives his motivations for committing the murder he is about to carry out. First, the requirements of traditional religion as revealed by the oracle of Apollo, and which are regularly associated with the demand for vengeance of the Erinyes, are cited but then at line 297 ff. an interesting set of additional motives is added. Here Orestes states that if he did not act under the stimulus of the Erinyes he would still have to carry out the killing of Clytemnestra for a number of very realistic and sophisticated reasons that are unrelated to the Erinyes. This second class of motivations include grief for his father, the pressure of poverty, and his feeling of patriotism that makes him unwilling to allow his fellow citizens who conquered Troy to remain servants of "two women" (297–304). By qualifying the reasons for Orestes' actions (joining the Erinyes to a series of very realistic motivations), Aeschylus gives us a clear and significant indication that he is not to be counted among the naïve believers in daemonic forces for, then, the mention of additional causes beyond the Erinyes would be quite unnecessary. This is a point that must be seriously considered in interpreting Aeschylus' general religious outlook. In the dramatic economy of this play, however, the Erinyes have a dominant and necessary role for reasons that will become clear from our analysis of the trilogy as a whole.

The vengeance theme of this play is clearly seen again in two statements of the chorus as it carries on its conversation with Orestes and Electra. At lines 306–14 the chorus asks that a "hateful word be accomplished in payment for a hateful word" and that Orestes pay back "a murderous blow for a murderous blow." The essential character of the concept of justice that is symbolized in this play is given its complete expression in the chorus' words "the doer must suffer, a thrice-old story announces this" (313–14). This point is supplemented by the chorus' remark at ll. 400–5 that it is the law that blood that has been spilled demands other blood in its place. This concept of justice is seen also in Orestes' speech at 434–38 where he indicates that his purpose is to make Clytemnestra pay for Agamemnon's death and then, with vengeance taken and his father's death requited, he is willing to die himself. The theme that blood must requite blood appears again in Orestes' speech at ll. 518–21. Here Orestes bitterly notes that the gifts sent by Clytemnestra are not equal to her crime, for all efforts, he says, expended because of murder are in vain. Clearly implicit here is the principle that is central to the symbolic meaning of the play—that blood must be paid for blood in equal amounts.

At ll. 523–50 we have another symbolic interlude similar in character to the recognition scene earlier and clearly differentiated from the intense realism of the *Agamemnon*. Here

Orestes interprets Clytemnestra's dream as a symbol of the guilt-retribution theme that has played a prominent role in the play so far. Introduction of the dream sequence has the advantage of lifting the action to a symbolic level so that we can examine its meaning independently from the psychological complexity of the characters. In this scene also vengeance emerges as the central motivating force in the play. This thought is further emphasized by the chorus at 11. 646–51 where it speaks of the Erinyes bringing back Orestes to exact payment for previous crime.

Clytemnestra's hypocrisy and essential guilt are shown clearly in her reaction to the disguised Orestes' report of his own "death." At 11. 707–18 Clytemnestra is sufficiently in control of herself after hearing of her son's supposed demise that she is able to make all necessary arrangements so that the "messenger's" night in the palace will be a comfortable one. Clytemnestra's "maternal love" is again exposed as a fraud and her remarkable self-control shows how little real affection she has for Orestes. The nurse's description of Clytemnestra at 11. 737–40 as hiding laughter behind a false gloom is further indication, if any is needed, of her guilt and hypocrisy.

Aegisthus' criminality, a theme closely associated with that of Clytemnestra's guilt, is underscored by the nurse at 1. 742 where she says, sadly, that he will rejoice in his heart when he hears the news of Orestes' "death" and at 11. 764–65 where she concludes her speech by saying she will now go to Aegisthus the "destroyer of the house" who will willingly learn her grievous news. The chorus also adds to this indictment of the current rulers when it refers at 1. 863 to Orestes' attempt to kindle a torchlight for freedom and the lawful rule of the state. Its fervent prayer for his victory at 1. 868 leaves no doubt where its sympathy lies.

At 1. 888 Clytemnestra again formally admits her guilt with a clear assertion that she slew Agamemnon with trickery. In the next line she asks for a "man-slaying axe" with which to defend herself from one who, she now knows, is her own son. This detail of action fits in well with the fuller picture that we have drawn of Clytemnestra as a figure of abnormal and unnatural violence and cruelty.

In the final confrontation between Clytemnestra and Orestes we see her marvelous skill at determining the course of events in the state put to its ultimate test. As Orestes closes in to pay her back, life for life, she makes the most ingeniously diabolical move available for her defense. She points to her breast as Orestes approaches and, reminding him that he took a mother's milk from her when he was a baby, asks if he can really kill her. Under the circumstances we can forgive Orestes for not examining the legitimacy of this claim now put forward by Clytemnestra, of loving and deserving motherhood, but some two hundred and fifty lines earlier we have had a detailed and highly realistic description given us by the old nurse who told us, in no uncertain terms, that it was she who nurtured and cared for the child "having received him from his mother" (750). The plea of her motherhood is the last desperate piece of lying hypocrisy that we are to hear from Clytemnestra in this play but it is the most telling argument she can muster at this point and it causes Orestes to falter, momentarily, as he sees himself driven outside the bounds of nature. The reflection offered by Pylades' warning that the god's will must be done finally, however, brings Orestes back to the point of resolute action.

The stichomythia which begins at 1. 908 and ends with Clytemnestra's death at 1. 930 clarifies beyond doubt the actual situation in regard to Clytemnestra's guilt and alleged justification for the murder of Agamemnon. Clytemnestra begins with a desperate plea, "I nurtured you—I wish to grow old with you" (908). Orestes spurns the logic of this argument by asking how the murderer of his father can live with him. Clytemnestra takes refuge here, as she has previously, when driven by accusing circumstances to a point of desperation, in fate as a motivating cause of the events that have happened. It is, however, highly significant to note that at this final moment of truth when her life is at stake Clytemnestra does not dare to cite the curse as the full cause of Agamemnon's death but rather calls it at 1. 910 a "partial cause" (παραιτία). If the curse is only a partial cause then Clytemnestra is clearly admitting that her own plots and ambitions are also a real element in any assessment of guilt and responsibility in this situation. Orestes now shows that he is fully aware of the hypocritical use of the curse by Clytemnestra as a shield to hide behind in the face of threatening vengeance and he answers her with perfect and appropriate irony that it is fate, then, that is responsible for her imminent death at his hands. And so it is, for fate is the "partial cause" (παραιτία) and common denominator of all events in human history; for the purposes, however, of assessing guilt or innocence it is not this factor which is of interest but rather the part of the total cause which we identify as human volition that is significant in our considerations. In the final play of the trilogy we return to this point at a more universal level which will have great importance for our interpretation of the *Oresteia* as a whole.

Our knowledge of Clytemnestra's cruelty and hypocrisy is increased when Orestes tells us in the course of his argument with her that though he was the son of a free father she sold him in a disgraceful fashion (915). When Clytemnestra slyly asks where the price is she got for him he replies, effectively, that he is ashamed to tell her (917) alluding to the illicit relationship of Clytemnestra and Aegisthus. Clytemnestra's only defense is to charge that Agamemnon committed similar indiscretions. To this Orestes replies that the case is different for a man caught in the hard toils of war and a woman living in comfortable leisure at home. Clytemnestra's weak reply (her strength for dispute seems to be ebbing now) is that it is hard for a woman to be without a man, a reply which, even when taken in its least odious sense, does little credit to her and places her as the polar opposite of a tradition best represented in Greek literature by Penelope. The verbal struggle reaches its climax at 1. 930, where the play's basic theme of blood for blood is restated in Orestes' line, "you slew whom you ought not slay, suffer what you ought not suffer." Agamemnon's murder has borne bitter but natural fruit in Clytemnestra's death at the hands of her son and we must automatically speculate on what is to come next.

The slaying of Clytemnestra and Aegisthus is greeted by the chorus as the means of escape from evils and from the wasting of the country's wealth by two polluted criminals (942–45). This thought is echoed at ll. 962–65 where the chorus bids the house, long downfallen, to rise up again.

Orestes then appears and displays with bitterness the trappings that Clytemnestra used when she killed Agamemnon (980 ff.). Here he calls attention to the vileness of Clytemnestra's deed and in so doing gives some necessary extenuation for the violent act that he has been driven to commit. Unnatural act of violence begets unnatural act of violence in the chain reaction of crime and vengeance which is illustrated in the first two plays of the *Oresteia*.

The murder of his mother, although in accordance with the principles of justice that dominate this play, is one that makes such overwhelming demands on Orestes' inner spirit that it begins to break under the strain. Aeschylus has very skillfully created a situation in which we can watch the demand of life for life, the demand for automatic vengeance operating under the most extreme conditions imaginable, where this judicial principle comes into conflict with one of the most basic and significant human relationships. The result of such conflict is the mental and spiritual disintegration which Orestes suffers at ll. 1021 ff. and which intensifies at l. 1048 where he sees terrifying forms that are invisible to the chorus and are described as "visions" by them at l. 1051. When Orestes insists on the threatening presence of these "visions" the chorus, taking a rationalistic view of his disturbance, cites as its cause the fresh blood on his hands which has driven him to the point of madness. Then, with the advice of the chorus, Orestes leaves the scene to seek divine aid for the plague, real or imaginary, that has beset him.

In the second act of the trilogy the principle of automatic vengeance, blood for blood, symbolized by the prominence of the Erinyes in the play, is invoked as the appropriate response to the crime committed in the *Agamemnon*. By placing this response in a context which demands violent and socially destructive reactions, Aeschylus enables us to test the adequacy of automatic vengeance in a critical way. The spiritual dilemma of Orestes at the end of the play and the fact that one murder for vengeance always contains within it the seed of a chain of similar murders are major signs of the inadequacy and disadvantages of vengeance as society's highest principle of justice. Thus at the end of the *Choephoroe* the solution of one problem has engendered others, equally grave, and we are left in a quandary from which it will be the duty of the trilogy's final play to deliver us. The *Eumenides* will sound the exultant note of the victory of human reason as the proper instrument for discriminating guilt and responsibility. In so doing, it will free man from servility to an only partially effective and barbarous means of maintaining the order of society and permit him to make his way toward that higher civilization and grander destiny of which it was Aeschylus' pride to be both poet and prophet.

3.

Apollo, Athena, and the Erinyes join together in the *Eumenides* to work out, on the symbolic level, the complex issues of individual guilt and social responsibility that have arisen in the earlier stages of the trilogy. The supernatural figures represent differing attitudes toward the question of justice on the human level and we may see in this play the ultimate solution to the problem of crime and vengeance that dominates the action of the *Oresteia*. To understand the meaning of the *Eumenides* as well as that of the trilogy as a whole we must make a careful analysis of the symbolic characteristics of the major figures in the play and of the plot in which they are involved. Before undertaking this, we should mention two aspects of the action of the *Eumenides* which have a bearing on more general interpretative considerations that have been discussed earlier.

The first of these considerations concerns one of the three

principal motifs which regularly appear in the plays of Aeschylus. This is the patriotic theme which celebrates the glory of Athens and which, although subordinated to the primary intellectual interest of the play, appears at frequent intervals in it. Instances of its occurrence can be seen at ll. 78–83, 287–91, 667–73, 757–66, 772–74, and 916–20 where poetic propaganda is made for the greatness of the historical city-state of Athens. These references take advantage of Orestes' Argive provenience to foreshadow the future history and advantages of Athenian-Argive relations and to give a basis for this relationship in ancient myth.

Secondly, and more specifically in regard to the *Oresteia*, is the line of action which carries forward our previous analysis of Clytemnestra's character and which clarifies our view of the severity of Orestes' crime by detailing the behavior of Clytemnestra's ghost when it first appears on the scene to rouse up the sleeping Erinyes. The ghost complains that it wanders shamefully among the dead who have neither forgotten nor forgiven the heinous murder of Agamemnon. Those who would defend or mitigate Clytemnestra's act will have to explain this deep, posthumous guilt and bitter ostracism which her ghost must endure.

To return now to the symbolic representation of the major characters in the play, it is clear that the first impression we get of the Erinyes is a distinctly unpleasant one. At ll. 46–56 the priestess of Apollo describes the physically disgusting appearance and disheveled dress of the band of Erinyes who have descended upon her temple. Apollo, god of the sun and archenemy of the darkness which the Erinyes inhabit, comments on their hateful nature which makes men, gods, and even wild beasts avoid them (69–73). The Erinyes thus are introduced in a way calculated to arouse an audience's violent distaste for them and we must keep this in mind together with other evidence as we assess the symbolic meaning of their role in the trilogy as a whole.

One of the most common points raised by the Erinyes as justification of their authority and mode of behavior is that they are ancient deities. There is an implication here that antiquity alone is a sufficient warrant for their rights and they use as terms of contempt the adjectives "young" and "new" which they apply to the Olympian gods. Thus the Erinyes come to stand in this play for the automatic, uncritical affirmation of ancient tradition and they view with horror and hatred any attempt to modify this principle in terms of more advanced ethical or legal doctrines. The Erinyes express this sense of their ancient honor and their anticipation of insult at the hands of the "young" gods at 11. 150 and 162. The point is made even more emphatic at 11. 171-72 where the Erinyes accuse Apollo of honoring men by destroying long-standing traditions that favor their authority. Here we may note with interest that in denouncing Apollo for honoring men the Erinyes ally themselves with the "misanthropy" of Zeus and Hermes in the *Prometheus Bound* while Athena and Apollo clearly share in Prometheus' famous "philanthropy." Thus in the two plays that are the climax of Aeschylus' art and thought, the *Prometheus Bound* and the *Eumenides*, there are both "progressive" and "reactionary" forces although the gods symbolizing them differ in each play. In the *Prometheus Bound*, which depicts the struggle of man's mind against nature, Zeus is the villain; but in the *Eumenides*, which celebrates the establishment of rational law in human society, Zeus stands in support of the deities who foster human progress. There is a consequent moral turnabout in the use of the adjectives "young" and "old." In the *Prometheus Bound* "young" and "new" are applied with scorn to Zeus and the Olympians by Prometheus who antedates them and intends in the future, as he has in the past, to modify their power by the strength of his intellect. In the *Eumenides* the "new" represents the progressive element in the play that triumphs over the crude and inadequate principles espoused by the guardians of the "old" order. Thus for Aeschylus the new divinities who come to be associated with the forces of nature still remain subject to the ancient and constantly operative power of the human mind. However, in matters of political and social organization old traditions have been superseded by the application of these same intellectual powers as man achieves more sophisticated control of his political and social environment. Thus "new" and "old" do not maintain a constant moral signification in the symbolism of Aeschylus' plays. What does remain constant, however, is the affirmation of man's intellect as the invincible instrument of human progress whether in the realm of nature or in the realm of society. The beneficiary of Aeschylus' most significant dramas is, then, man in all the bright splendor of his great intellectual victories and we shall have occasion to speak of this point again when we come to the final summing up of the achievement of Aeschylus.

The characterization of the Erinyes on the basis of their disgusting appearance and habits is continued in Apollo's angry address to them at ll. 179–97. He demands that this awful body quit his temple for they might appropriately inhabit a lion's den, not the seat of his prophetic utterances. The picture he presents of the Erinyes vomiting forth clots of blood which they have sucked up from the slain (ll. 181–84) evokes, effectively, the feeling of loathing and disgust that we have already been asked to feel toward the fearful goddesses.

Apollo's attitude toward the Erinyes is further seen in his statement that they are not fit to enter his temple (207) and in the sarcasm with which he inquires into their "noble privileges" as exactors of vengeance (209). At ll. 211–24 Apollo points out serious weaknesses in the approach of the Erinyes to the problem of justice. First and foremost, the actions of the Erinyes are inconsistent as their vengeance is applied automatically against Orestes without proper consideration of the nature of Clytemnestra's crime and its role as a causal agent in his act. Apollo points out that Agamemnon has as much right to their protection as Clytemnestra and in this inconsistency of approach we see the basic inadequacy of the Erinyes' attitude to justice among men. The new justice of the "young" gods must be something of universal application that can be consistently applied without leading to self-contradiction, absurdity, or a continuation of a state of evil and injustice. The Erinyes cannot see this abstract conception of justice and base their inconsistent action on the traditional view that the murder of someone of related blood is a greater criminal act than any other form of murder. Apollo's arguments in this passage are tending toward a much more rational and modern conception of justice in which reason determines that all individuals have an equal stake in protection from homicide and which rejects the automatic invocation of traditional religious dogma as the basis of a system of justice. Universal application of a rationalized system of justice is essentially Apollo's program and he significantly awaits its carrying out in Pallas' city (224).

At ll. 244–53 we see the Erinyes pursuing Orestes with the primitive, animal-like behavior that characterizes their brand of justice. They compare themselves to dogs tracking a deer (246) and then proudly state that the smell of human blood brings laughter to their lips (253). There should be no doubt that we are meant to reject, strongly, the primitive type of justice espoused by this abominable, animalistic band of deities.

At l. 350 we get another significant indication of the ostracism and isolation of the Erinyes from the society of the "young" gods who now hold power. They tell us here that no other god shares in their feasts or associates with them and there should be no difficulty in assessing the symbolic meaning of this fact. At ll. 363–64 we learn that Zeus has rejected the company of the Erinyes and this is another indication of their lowly position among the gods and a strong additional suggestion that we are to hold the Erinyes, in their present condition and state of mind, in contempt.

At l. 426 Athena makes a point in her discussion with the Erinyes that strongly symbolizes the difference of approach of the "new, young" Olympian gods from that of the ancient band of vengeance seekers. She inquires here, in response to the flat accusation of matricide leveled at Orestes by the Erinyes, if he committed the crime out of fear or under some duress. Thus Athena shows that she is preoccupied with the subtleties of cause and motivation in weighing a question of guilt and innocence while the Erinyes are interested only in an automatic response which because it is uncritical, irrational, and inequitably applied must lead to a significant form of injustice. The Erinyes are not capable of appreciating the rational distinctions of Athena and they cannot accept any justification of Orestes' act. Athena continues her more sophisticated procedure by demanding to hear both sides of the case in order to assess all evidence. She clearly shows her contempt for the inadequacy of the Erinyes' approach to Orestes' situation when she says at 1. 430 that they are more interested in the formal conduct of the trial than in the actual achievement of justice. Here the issue between the Erinyes and Athena and Apollo is again clearly seen. The Erinyes operate on the basis of traditional formulae in an automatic way; the Olympians are made to stand for a rational, thorough investigation of cause and motive where all elements are weighed and balanced before a judicial decision is made. Justice for the Erinyes is the automatic application of formulaic vengeance in response to specified criminal acts. As such, the Erinyes' concept of justice is rigid and external while that maintained by Athena and Apollo is subtle and adaptive, taking into consideration the complexities of the human situation. Under this approach, as Athena warns the Erinyes, appeals to formula and tradition will not be tolerated if they allow the unjust to conquer the just (432).

Orestes gives a defense of himself, at this point, that is calculated to appeal to the rationalistic conception of justice of the Olympian gods. He describes again, in detail, the vicious crime of Clytemnestra and indicates that an act of such enormity demanded punishment which under the prevailing conditions fell to his responsibility to carry out. Orestes buttresses his argument with an appeal to the oracles of Apollo and in so severe a situation as matricide the need to cite sanction from divine quarters can easily be understood. An additional example of divine acceptance of co-responsibility is found at 11. 576–81.

Athena finds the matter a difficult one to decide even with

all of the advantages afforded by her godhead. She must mediate between the ancient and powerful forces represented by the Erinyes and the newer, more sophisticated forces she and Apollo symbolize. Her problem derives from the fact that although the forces represented by the Erinyes are too clumsy and primitive to provide a fully adequate form of justice, they nevertheless must be recognized as important and necessary elements in the maintenance of order in any state. Athena's real difficulty is to find a way, not of eliminating these forces, but of diverting them into socially beneficial channels.

Athena arrives at a two-part solution to the critical problem she faces. First she establishes the Council of the Areopagus as a court of homicide "for all time" (484). The establishment of this human court is symbolic of one of the most dramatic steps forward in the development of human civilization: the substitution of a rational body, weighing and balancing motives and evidence in an overriding spirit of equity that is sensitive to significant nuances of human behavior, for the primitive appeal to dogmatic religious doctrine as an undeviating, monolithic principle of judicial action. The human judges on the Council of the Areopagus must, perforce, like Apollo and Athena, examine by rational means the evidence of fact and motivation and come to a decision in each individual case on the basis of this rational process. The automatic, primitive demand of "blood for blood" must necessarily cease for as long as the Council of the Areopagus has tenure, that is, "for all time." Thus the new principle of rationalized justice is given an institutional embodiment in the form of the most ancient and respected court in Athens.

The second part of Athena's solution occupies the last quarter of the play where she finds a way of integrating the Erinyes into a society that has just taken a major step forward by attaining to a system of rationalized justice. We will see in detail, later, the specific ways in which Athena wins the favor of the Erinyes for Athens. In order, however, to understand the full implications of the two-part solution of Athena we must anticipate here some subsequent developments in the text. At 1.

698 Athena counsels her citizens not to cast "the fearful" completely out of the city for it is a necessary, although not in itself sufficient, support for justice in any society. Here we see the essential usefulness of the Erinyes even in the most highly sophisticated society; they will be guarantors of an elemental fear of vengeance that acts as a buttress for the fully developed system of justice which nourishes the existence of any successful state. In the *Eumenides*, then, Aeschylus has boldly symbolized the great revolution that took place when man cloaked the principle of elemental fear in the apparatus of rationalized justice for the purpose of reordering society to his advantage. This glowing faith in the power of the human intellect as a guiding force in man's political and social domain is matched, as we shall see in the next chapter, by an equally exuberant affirmation of the ability of the human intellect to deal effectively with the forces of external nature which plays a central role in the symbolic meaning of the *Prometheus Bound*.

At l. 490 the Erinyes begin an ode in which they declare that society will collapse if the principle of vengeance for which they stand is not respected. They see no possible alternative or improvement to their brand of justice and can only conceive of a vacuum appearing if the rule of "blood for blood" is abrogated. We are now aware that by the end of the play the view of justice maintained by the Erinyes will be swept away by a new form of rationalized justice which, balancing nuances of motive and cause, can eliminate or modify many of the socially injurious consequences of the more primitive type of justice.

As the trial of Orestes proceeds, Apollo is called upon to defend the slaying of Clytemnestra. This he does on the basis of a number of considerations at ll. 614–66. Apollo explicitly argues that Agamemnon was killed by treachery on his return from heroic exploits at Troy. The contrast between the noble stature of Agamemnon and the foul and criminal conditions under which he was killed make his murder an atrocity.

Implicit here is the judgment that Clytemnestra's death, terrible as the act of matricide is, resulted from considerations of necessary and justified punishment in view of the character of the criminal act she had committed. The "new" justice is at work aiming at an adequate solution to the successive outbursts of violence that continue to unsettle the stability of the state.

To this approach the chorus of Erinyes responds with an appeal to tradition as opposed to the principles of rationalized justice. To support their position the Erinyes cite Zeus's cruel treatment of his own father as "proof" that he would not side with the father against the mother (640–43). This old-fashioned and dogmatic type of thinking is met by Apollo with anger but also with the rational argument that Zeus only bound up his father, and there is a way out of chains, but there is no possible return from the death Agamemnon suffered (644–51). The Erinyes' appeal to authority is here contrasted with a procedure that draws logical and ethical distinctions.

Apollo musters a counter argument against the Erinyes at this point which sounds strange to modern ears. We recall that he had already used a rational approach when he argued that on the basis of motivation Orestes' act was more justified than Clytemnestra's. Now frustrated in his attempt to score a point by a rational approach, he cites a doctrine that directly contradicts the "anti-paternal" argument used by the Erinyes a few lines earlier. In exasperation with the irrationality of the Erinyes he dogmatically announces his support for the doctrine that the mother is not really a parent of the child but that only the father has a right to this title (657–61), an assumption which would greatly alter the character of Orestes' crime. We know that a similar doctrine of parental relationships was expressed by Anaxagoras and we have good reason to believe that Aeschylus was acquainted with, and influenced by, pre-Socratic thought. If there really is a pre-Socratic echo here then we have an interesting situation in which the dogmatic appeal to ancient tradition is met by Apollo with an appeal to a doctrine of one of the most advanced thinkers of the contemporary Greek world.⁶ At any event, since reason has no effect here, Apollo's dogmatic citation of this principle is an effective rejoinder to the refuge the Erinyes regularly take in ancient tradition.

At ll. 681–706 we have Athena's praise for the Council of the Areopagus and the important role it will play in the Athenian state. Reverence and fear will be associated with this body and these two emotions Athena tells us are the basis of just actions among the citizens. The state is to steer a middle course between anarchy and despotism on the grounds of its respect and fear of the law. We have already discussed the significant place which Athena here gives to "the fearful" and, consequently, the important place in the state which the Erinyes are still to play when and if they adopt a positive and beneficial attitude toward the state.

The Erinyes warn that their ancient rights must be respected, harping on traditional considerations that have played so essential a role in their claims up to this point (731–33). Irritated, we may believe, by her failure to impress the Erinyes with earlier rationalistic argumentation, Athena has recourse to the same type of dogmatic assertion that characterizes the Erinyes' claims and which we have seen Apollo use when his reasoned arguments made no headway against the tradition-oriented thought of the Erinyes. She justifies her support of

---

6. The thesis argued in the *Eumenides* that the mother is not the parent of the child has been connected by some scholars with a doctrine Aristotle attributes to Anaxagoras in *De Generatione Animalium* IV, ii, 763 B 30–34. For a discussion of this point as well as reference to a contrary point of view on this connection between Aeschylus and Anaxagoras see B. Gladigow, "Aischylos und Heraklit," *Archiv für Geschichte der Philosophie*, N.S. XLIV (1962), 226–39. Gladigow discusses several ways in which Heracleitean influence can be seen in Aeschylus and refers to works by Jaeger and other scholars (pp. 226–27) that argue for pre-Socratic influence on Aeschylus. Such an influence is exactly what we would expect if Aeschylus actually is the intellectually progressive thinker that we have found him to be in our analysis of his work. Jaeger's judgment, quoted by Gladigow (p. 226), provides welcome support for this view. Jaeger writes, "Eine solche direkte Einwirkung moderner philosophischer Spekulation und anderer neugewonnener Erkenntnisse zeigt sich auch sonst bei dem Dichter."

Orestes by calling attention to her closer connection to the male rather than to the female as evidenced by her remarkable birth. Athena, like Apollo, can fight fire with fire.

After the formal acquittal of Orestes the Erinyes begin a long series of laments (778) in which they deplore the loss of their power and threaten permanent enmity to Athens. Athena responds in various ways to the angry outbursts of the Erinyes. First she attempts to mollify them by pointing out that the votes were equal in the case and that for this reason they suffered no dishonor since it was Zeus's will that brought about Orestes' victory (ll. 794–99). The closeness of the vote symbolizes the important and necessary place the Erinyes must have in any state as guardians of a proper fear and respect for law and authority. We have mentioned this point earlier where we noted that the Erinyes are not, however, a sufficient support for the legal and political institutions of a really advanced society. Athena then holds out the promise of great honors for the Erinyes if they accept a new role as protective deities in the state (804–7). Their continued anger forces Athena to try another tack and at ll. 824–31 she threatens them with violent punishment if they continue their wrath at Athens. She couples these threats, again, with promises of rewards and offerings of the first fruits of sacrifices (834–36).

Not easily persuaded, the Erinyes continue to lament their painful situation and the ill-treatment they feel they have suffered. Patiently, Athena seeks to win them over by emphasizing the honored place they will have in the state if they abandon their hostility (846–69) and her efforts, after much argument, are finally crowned with success at ll. 892–902. There the Erinyes, no longer bemoaning their wounded dignity, begin to assert their willingness to accept the terms offered by Athena which include authority over the general prosperity of the state. The long struggle between these mighty antagonists may be understood as the poet's dramatic symbol of the difficult and extended process that must have taken place, historically, when the ancient religious law of blood guilt and pollution merged with the new, more rational legal concepts which began to arise in Athens at the end of the seventh century B.C. With harmony restored again between the "old" and the "new" gods, the action of the play reaches its culmination in the sounding of a proud, patriotic note as the Erinyes praise Athens as the city honored by Ares and Zeus.

The series of events which had its source in Clytemnestra's impassioned murder of Agamemnon now reaches its climax in the joyous, lyric acceptance by the Erinyes of a new and powerful role in society. We have traveled a path which saw the egoistical assertion of individual desire fail as a secure, guiding principle of society; we have seen how "blood for blood" as the basis for a system of law contained within it the seeds of continuing violence and social destruction; and now we have arrived at the point of establishing an effective solution to the problem of justice within a state which is the central political theme of the trilogy. At the end of the *Eumenides*, the ancient function of the Erinyes, that of awing men into a paralyzing fear of vengeance, is significantly modified, but not eliminated. This is accomplished by placing it in the context of new responsibilities for the general prosperity of the people and by winning from the Erinyes a tacit recognition of the powers of the Council of the Areopagus which will exercise its authority "for all time."

A primitive but necessary fear and a system of rationalized justice that depends upon the application of the highest human intellectual powers are married in the *Eumenides* and the bright ode of joy and reconciliation that springs up from the smiling lips of the once gloomy Erinyes and the once troubled Athena tells us what an important and blessed event this is.[7]

7. Again we find ourselves in agreement with several points of Sidgwick's analysis of the play that are presented in his edition of the *Eumenides* (Oxford, 1927) 15–17. He writes:

"The Erinyes, though Orestes must be saved from their anger, are yet not evil. To fear them, to worship them, is needful for man's material welfare and still more for his moral health. . . . To the moral interest of the play, thus strongly sustained and brought to an impressive and triumphant close, all else is subordinate. But hardly less exciting and moving to an Athenian would be the political and patriotic interest. The gods in releasing Orestes make use of a human instrument; and Athena naturally chooses for this transcendent honour the ancient and sacred court of Areiopagos, close to her own citadel. It was the common and natural instinct of antiquity to ascribe revered institutions to a divine origin. But that tame phrase helps us very little to realise the thrill of pleasure, pride, and reverence with which the Athenians of 458 would see the actual founding, by Athena herself, of their immemorial court take place on the stage before their eyes. . . .

"As to the mention of the Argive alliance (289–762), that is only in a passing allusion: it is indeed an exceedingly happy and natural touch of skill that Orestes the Argive in vowing eternal thanks to Athens should use words which bear a double reference to the audience: and which dignify current politics by linking them thus to the heroic past."

The general interpretation of the *Oresteia* that is presented in this book is in close harmony with certain of Karl Reinhardt's remarks on the *Eumenides* in *Aischylos als Regisseur und Theologe* (Bern, 1949) pp. 140–41. He states that, "Eins nur scheint uns anzusprechen als etwas noch immer Gültiges: eine Idee des Fortschritts oder, sagen wir, der Überwindung, Überführung und Bewahrung alter Furcht und alten Schauders im Bestand des neuen staatlichen Gemeinschaft." The view presented here is also in harmony with much in the summary of the standard scholarly interpretations of the *Eumenides* that Reinhardt gives in this passage. Finally, with his remark that "aber das Alte ist im Neuen wieder nicht vernichtet, sondern darein eingegangen," the interpretation of the symbolic meaning of the *Eumenides* presented in this book is in full agreement.

CHAPTER FIVE

RELIGIOUS DRAMA

1.

THE MOST IMPORTANT PROBLEM THAT FACES THE STUDENT OF Aeschylus is to define the poet's conception of Zeus: for in Aeschylus' religious thought are his most profound reflections on the nature and meaning of human existence. Interpreters of Aeschylus' theology encounter a major and deep-seated difficulty in an apparent ambivalence of the poet's view of Zeus that ranges from his representation of a reverent chorus in the *Suppliants* praying to Zeus as the "lord of lords, most blessed of the blessed and most perfect power of the perfect," (524–27) to his depiction of mocking contempt for the great Olympian god expressed in Prometheus' defiant words, "nothing is less a care to me than Zeus" (*Prometheus Bound*, 938). We must investigate this apparently contradictory attitude toward Zeus to see whether it results from a basic confusion or inadequacy in the religious philosophy of the poet or whether, at a deeper level, it harbors within it a perceptive and truly unified conception of divinity. The first step in our procedure will be to examine the nature of Zeus as it is presented in the *Suppliants* and the *Prometheus Bound*, two plays in which we have indicated that the portrayal of Zeus offers a difficulty of interpretation.

Zeus appears in the *Suppliants* most impressively and most frequently in the role of the protector of the weak and innocent. In nearly every line addressed by the fearful chorus of Danaids to him there is some explicit or implicit recognition of the protective power of Zeus. The very first line of the play sounds the keynote of this theme as the chorus names Zeus the protector of suppliants. In addition, in their opening song they call upon him as their savior (26) and as the guardian (26) of pious men. He is also pictured as a deity from whom those in need may expect pity (210) and he is assigned the important role of rendering final judgment (231) on the dead for their crimes. Emphatically Zeus is described by the Danaids as a wrathful god toward those who mistreat the suppliant and it is in his avenging anger (347, 646) that they see their protection against strong and brutal adversaries. The great might and authority of this Zeus is celebrated by the chorus when it sings, "What without you is fulfilled for man?" (823–24). Thus the Zeus of this play is the protector of the weak, the avenger of the wronged, and a towering symbol of the ultimate triumph of justice in the world.

When we turn to the *Prometheus Bound* we find a radically different attitude toward Zeus than the one which prevailed in the *Suppliants*. Hephaestus, who reluctantly binds Prometheus under the command of Zeus, terms his master "harsh" (35) while the chorus of Oceanids informs us that the Zeus of this play rules in a despotic fashion (150) under new laws. This Zeus as opposed to the Zeus of the *Suppliants* lacks pity and is described by the chorus as cruel and "hard hearted" (160). Furthermore the chorus warns Prometheus that the Zeus who persecutes him, like most tyrants, has a mind that is not open to reason (185). Prometheus charges Zeus with ingratitude as well as cruelty when he reminds the chorus that he now suffers so shamefully despite the fact that it was he who helped Zeus attain his present power. The Zeus of this play, cruel, tyrannical, and ungrateful, is also presented as the hater and not the protector of mankind, for we are told that it was Prometheus' successful defiance of Zeus which saved mankind from destruction. With the introduction of Io into the story the character of Zeus's cruelty is further emphasized. Zeus in his lust for Io has subjected her to a life of torment which Prometheus outlines in all of its painful detail. Yet throughout this description of Zeus's tyranny and cruelty there runs another, counter theme, the ultimate limitation of Zeus's power. In an important interchange between Prometheus and the chorus the god declares that Zeus cannot escape what has been fated (518) but even more significant is the emphasis throughout the play on the fact that Prometheus has the power to check Zeus's will. It was Prometheus who saved mankind in opposition to Zeus, and it is Prometheus who has the secret knowledge which Zeus must learn if he is to maintain his power. Finally, it is Prometheus who scorns the savage threats carried by Hermes from Zeus and who unflinchingly defies his tormentor. Zeus is mighty but he cannot make Prometheus speak against his will.

Thus we have two characterizations of Zeus. The Zeus of the *Suppliants* is man's protector, the stern but just judge of good and evil, the guardian of the suppliant and the stranger, whereas the Zeus of the *Prometheus Bound* is a cruel tyrant, a hater of mankind who exercises his savage power without respect to justice. How are we to reconcile the existence in a single god of characteristics so widely divergent?

In previous studies of this problem several explanations have been suggested for Zeus's dual personality. H. W. Smyth has argued that Aeschylus "operates with divine as well as with human characters; he is not bound by any ecclesiastical prescription to any fixed conception even of the one highest god, toward whom his religious aspiration darkly moves. Once Zeus enters into the domain of mythology, ever fluctuating, ever inconsistent, for the depiction of character he is no more than human."[1]

Under this analysis the charge of simple, almost whimsical

1. H. W. Smyth, *Aeschylean Tragedy* (Berkeley, 1924), p. 62.

inconsistency is leveled at Zeus or perhaps at Aeschylus himself. Zeus, however, is far too majestic a god and Aeschylus far too capable a poet to be convicted of this fault. Aeschylus, in fact, saw deep, powerful reasons for the ambiguity of Zeus's relationship to the world and these reasons must be sought in the interpretation which Aeschylus has made of the universe around him.[2]

Smyth, however, has also offered a more significant explanation for the diversity in Zeus's character. This explanation, which may be called the "Evolutionary Theory" of Zeus's character, is expressed by Smyth as follows: "There are not wanting elsewhere in Aeschylus indications of the conception of the perfectioning of the crude mythological Zeus into the

2. More sophisticated theories which also assume a certain type of inconsistency in Zeus have been developed by K. Reinhardt, *Aischylos als Regisseur und Theologe* (Bern, 1949), pp. 64–76 and H. Lloyd-Jones, "Zeus in Aeschylus," *JHS*, LXXVI (1956), 55–67. In explaining the duality of Zeus's character Reinhardt, who does not consider the evidence from the *Suppliants*, maintains that there is a mysterious coexistence of opposites in the world and that it is thus understandable that we should find contradictory qualities in Zeus's nature. The following quotations from his argument outline his position: "Bei Hesiod ist alles unverrückbar. Jeder Gott hat seinen Ort und Wert im Kosmos seines festgefügten Alls. Bei Aischylos hat selbst das Höchste, Heiligste die Fähigkeit, zweideutig, wechselnd widersprüchlich, unsinnig zu werden. Eine höhere und geheime Ordnung wird verdeckt von einer in die Sichtbarkeit gerückten . . . Den Göttern eigen ist nicht, das sie sich entwickeln, sondern das sie zwei Gesichter zeigen [pp. 70–71] . . . Allerdings hat Aischylos die Gegensätze nicht erfunden . . . Aber erst bei Aischylos durchdringen sie das ganze Reich des Religiösen [p. 73] . . . Denn gegeben mit der gleichen Grundform ist stets auch die Umkehr und der Gegensatz [p. 76]." The difficulty with Reinhardt's view is that it does not analyze Aeschylus' approach to this dualistic universe nor does it tell us what role the poet assigned to man under these conditions. Aeschylus is far more specific than Reinhardt about the nature of the dualistic universe in which man dwells. Lloyd-Jones portrays Zeus as an arbitrary and inconsistent god when he writes (p. 66) that "the gods by their laws encourage righteousness among men. But they themselves are not obliged to obey those laws, nor should we be reasonable to expect it" and (p. 67) that "Zeus is indeed the champion of Dike, a rough retributive justice; he insists that men, like gods, shall keep his law." Here Zeus is presented as a god who arbitrarily does and does not follow the principles of justice. As is argued in this paper, such inconsistency is not appropriate to Zeus's important role as the king of gods and men.

Zeus of a spiritual religion. . . . Aeschylus is in fact an evolutionist as regards both gods and man." [3]

This view wins the support of Gilbert Murray who argues that Zeus is a god who "learns and grows" and whose striving "becomes more intelligent, and at last more spiritual." [4]

This "Evolutionary Theory," however, entails some serious difficulties. Let us see how the evolutionists explain the change in Zeus's character which they claim takes place between the dramatic dates of the *Prometheus Bound* and the *Suppliants*. Smyth states: "As Prometheus had been softened in course of time, so a change has come upon his antagonist who is under bonds to Fate. Right has been added unto might. Mercy and equity temper the omnipotence of Zeus; he has learned to recognize the inherent justice of Prometheus' championship of man now ennobled through the providence of the ancient rebel to his rule." [5]

Murray urges, "First, Zeus has the power of Thought, the power of Learning by experience, which differentiates him and his rule from all that has gone before. He has also led man along the road of Thought. He learns and does better." [6]

The difficulty with both of the above interpretations is that no textual evidence is cited in support of them. Where does Aeschylus say that Zeus learns mercy, equity, and justice, or give his warrant to the statement that "Zeus learns and does better?" If Aeschylus is, indeed, an evolutionist in regard to Zeus's character then surely there must be some words of his own to prove the point and show how a god whose entire career has been based on violence learns to be merciful and how he, when compelled to compromise with a lesser deity by most dire necessity, learns justice from this experience. The text of Aeschylus, as I read it, is bare of any information on these points but it does contain evidence that contradicts the evolutionary hypothesis. At lines 907–27 in *Prometheus Bound*

3. Smyth, *Aeschylean Tragedy*, p. 120.
4. G. Murray, *Aeschylus: The Creator of Tragedy* (Oxford, 1940), p. 110.
5. Smyth, *Aeschylean Tragedy*, pp. 120–21.
6. Murray, *The Creator of Tragedy*, p. 108.

Aeschylus has Prometheus speak in detail of the future that awaits Zeus. Here Prometheus, who knows so well the chain of events that will bring Zeus to his knees, knows nothing of any evolution in his character. Yet here, if anywhere, is the appropriate moment for Aeschylus to announce the eventual conversion of Zeus. Instead, we have a picture of a god who will act in the future exactly as he has in the past until he learns that he must submit to superior force. This, however, is a truth which he already knew for he had taught it to his own father, Kronos. Thus, though the evolutionists claim that Zeus will undergo a soul-deep moral conversion, all Aeschylus says is that he will yield to necessity.[7]

7. For criticism of the evolutionary theory see Reinhardt (*Aischylos als Regisseur und Theologe*, pp. 68–76) and Lloyd-Jones ("Zeus in Aeschylus," pp. 57, 66). In specific refutation of the alleged evolution in Zeus's character in the Prometheus trilogy, Lloyd-Jones perceptively remarks (pp. 66–67): "We know . . . that Zeus did not suffer destruction; and we may therefore easily infer that it was by revealing the secret that Prometheus purchased his release. Now if Zeus has in the meantime reformed in character, it is odd that he should need the threat of impending disaster to lead him to pardon his noble adversary; this argument . . . surely confirms arguments against believing that Prometheus owed his release to a change of heart on the part of Zeus which I set out earlier. The change of attitude by the *Eumenides* is indeed a parallel, but one which indicates the opposite of what it has often been supposed to. The Eumenides do not change their character, but they do a deal with Athene, and in consequence their attitude changes. So, I suggest, must Zeus have done a deal with Prometheus, and changed his attitude in consequence." Despite the difficulties involved in it, the evolutionary theory, in some form, has been accepted by many scholars as the explanation of the contradictory aspects of Zeus's character. Thus Wilamowitz, who was attempting to explain how the cruel Zeus of the *Prometheus Bound* was transformed into the merciful god of the lost sequel, is quoted by Reinhardt (*Aischylos als Regisseur und Theologe*, p. 68), as follows: "Über die Anstösse, die sich daraus ergeben, dass der erste Gott mit dem zweiten identisch sein soll, kann ich nur wieder und wieder sagen: es gilt die Lösung, die Friedrich Vischer für die Grausamkeiten des Judengottes im Alten Testamente gibt: Da war der liebe Gott selbst noch jung." In dealing with the same problem F. Solmsen, *Hesiod and Aeschylus* (Ithaca, 1949), p. 164, writes: "Between *Prometheus Bound* and the second or, possibly, third play of the same trilogy Zeus himself has gone the way that leads to 'understanding' and therefore may escape the threat to his continued rule which Prometheus has learnt from Gaea."

A third explanation for the apparent contradiction in Zeus's character has also been offered by Murray. He suggests that there may be some ultimate mystery to the nature of Zeus which is too deep for man to fathom. Thus what may seem like evil to us or to Prometheus or to Io may in the final analysis by otherwise. On this view, according to Murray, the actions of Zeus are "inscrutable by our mortal minds and therefore unjudgeable." [8] This position, suggested by Murray's study of the Book of Job, may well be valid for the ultimate Zeus who is beyond human ken; we are not, however, dealing with this unknowable divinity here, but with Aeschylus' *conception* of the character of the supreme god of the Greek pantheon. In the *Prometheus Bound* Aeschylus repeatedly calls Zeus a cruel tyrant and unequivocally condemns his treatment of Prometheus and Io. In the *Suppliants* the chorus sings gracious praise of the justice and goodness of Zeus. Since Aeschylus believes he knows Zeus well enough to praise and blame him he cannot be asking us to consider Zeus an ineffably mysterious being. Rather he is presenting a deity whose actions stem from some striking ambiguity of attitude toward the world. The complexity of Zeus's character and the apparent contradiction of his actions make him a difficult god to understand, but Aeschylus does not suggest, as Sophocles does in the *Oedipus Tyrannus*, that it is not within the power of human intelligence to grasp the meaning of the divine will.

If, then, Zeus is too formidable and impressive a god to be simply an inconsistent character, if all of the evidence from the *Prometheus Bound* indicates that Zeus will remain a tyrant who yields only to superior force, and if Aeschylus, himself, makes no suggestion about any unfathomable mystery enveloping divine activity, we must seek to understand the variation in Zeus's character in a way different from any of those discussed above.

We must first ask how Aeschylus came to his conception of Zeus. Since from all we know of Aeschylus' life he was not a mystic, it is unlikely that his view of Zeus was formed through

---

8. Murray, *The Creator of Tragedy*, p. 109.

some type of divine revelation. Rather, Aeschylus was a creative artist and we must try to comprehend the process by which such an artist comes to understand the world in which he lives. If we reject mysticism, then the world view of the artist, like that of the ordinary man, must be derived from his experiences in daily life. Aeschylus' Zeus, who represents the supernatural force that gives meaning and purpose to the world, is, in all probability, an extrapolation from the poet's experience of the nature of the universe around him. If it is reasonable to suppose that Aeschylus' conception of Zeus is based on his experience in life then it is also reasonable that we should try to define these experiences from the evidence in the two plays before us and thus gain a better understanding of the complex Aeschylean view of Zeus.

In both the *Suppliants* and in the *Prometheus Bound* Zeus is pictured as a reigning monarch, although in the former play he remains at a great distance from the action,[9] while in the latter he is very close to being an actual character in the play since the entire drama is based on his uncompromising conflict with Prometheus. The Zeus who rules over the universe in the *Suppliants* is the model of the good king. We have seen that he is fair, just, and a source of protection for the innocent who are oppressed. In short this Zeus possesses all the characteristics of the virtuous political state. It is likely that Aeschylus learned the nature of this Zeus from the ideals of his native city of Athens. Thus I would call the Zeus of this play the Zeus of the Polis. Zeus, however, rules the universe of the *Prometheus Bound* in a very different way from that of the *Suppliants*. In the *Prometheus Bound* Zeus, although he never actually appears on stage, makes his presence felt in many ways. His character and his power are the subject of the conversation that begins the play in which Hephaestus, Cratos, and Bia take part. He is described at length in the conversations which Prometheus has with Oceanus and Io. However, he comes

---

9. The fact that the girls call upon Zeus even when they are not sure he will listen to them (168 ff.) indicates how distant and impersonal a force he is in this play.

closest to personal involvement in the action and makes his influence most vividly felt in the play at lines 1080 ff. when he strikes the still defiant Prometheus with the full might of his vengeance. Here Zeus forces Prometheus to endure the destructive violence of earthquake (1081), crashing thunder (1083), flaming lightning (1084), and the wild storms that sweep the land and sea (1084-88). The god who calls these forces into action is clearly the lord of all the destructive powers in nature. We recall, in addition, that Zeus is regularly described in this play as "savage," "cruel," and "arbitrary" and that these are the customary attributes of the forces of nature,[10] such as those mentioned above, which constantly intervene in the settled existence of man and leave his accomplishments a shambles. Thus I would call the arbitrary despot of the *Prometheus Bound*, who commands these terrifying forces, the Zeus of Nature in that he symbolizes the uncontrolled, destructive powers in the world just as the god whom I call the Zeus of the Polis symbolizes the controlled, creative activity of the just state. Aeschylus had seen the ambitious struggles of men flower into great achievement in his own Athens. He recognized that a basic condition of the success of the state was its observation of the principles of justice and the performance of its religious obligations. Therefore, he made Zeus a grand symbol of all of the spiritual forces that reach majestic fulfillment in the creation of the polis, and it is this Zeus that Aeschylus portrays in the *Suppliants*. However, Aeschylus also knew that man's cultural and political accomplishments could be wiped out at a moment's notice by the unreasoning forces of nature. The events of life are linked together for Aeschylus as they are at that dramatic point in

10. The adjective τραχύς which is used of Zeus in the *Prometheus Bound* at 11. 35, 186, and 324 is applied to natural phenomena in the same play at 11. 726 and 1048. Descriptive words and phrases similar in spirit to τραχύς such as ἀθέτως κρατύνει (150), πλησικάρδιος (160), ἀκίχητα ... ἤθεα ... κέαρ ἀπαράμυθον (184-85) are too anthropomorphic to be applied to nature. They add, however, to the characterization given Zeus by the repeated use of τραχύς and strengthen the impression of harshness and cruelty that both Zeus and nature share as a prime characteristic.

Thucydides where Pericles' joyous praise of Athens fades directly into a depiction of the macabre events of Athens' great plague. Because the destructive forces of nature are also an all too real part of life, Aeschylus made Zeus symbolic of them in his characterization of this god in the *Prometheus Bound*. Thus Aeschylus' two views of Zeus are a poetic recognition of opposed forces in the world itself. His conception of Zeus is very different from that of Sophocles' Apollo in the *Oedipus Tyrannus* who, enveloped in mystery, dwells beyond the world. Aeschylus' Zeus, on the contrary, is immanent within the world since he is no more, nor less, than a symbol of all of the world's forces, both creative and destructive.

We shall now discuss the important implications of this view for man, since every attempt by man to understand his gods includes the hope of discovering his own place in the world. The Zeus of the *Suppliants* symbolizes justice, piety, and those other virtues which make the political state viable; the state, in turn, provides the framework in which man's intellectual and artistic achievements can unfold. Wherever man establishes a state he announces his intention to wrest a place for himself from a hostile nature. Thus the Zeus of the *Suppliants* under whose aegis alone the state can prosper and mankind progress is a principal source of hope among men just as the Zeus of the *Prometheus Bound* with his cruel and tyrannical behavior is the chief source of pessimism among them. The problem which man faces, therefore, is to increase the protective power of the Zeus of the *Suppliants* and to diminish the destructive force of the Zeus of the *Prometheus Bound*. The question is whether it is in man's capability to do this. Aeschylus' answer is a firm Yes.

In the *Prometheus Bound*, as we have seen, mention was often made of some remarkable limitation on the power of Zeus. Zeus must obey what has been fated but, even more important, he must eventually yield to Prometheus if he is to maintain his rule. In this representation of Zeus forced to reach a compromise with Prometheus we begin to see a way in which the gap between the Zeus of the *Prometheus Bound*, Zeus the Destroyer, and the Zeus of the *Suppliants*, Zeus the Protector, may be bridged. We are told that Zeus the great, savage, unpredictable lord of nature must some day bend his knee to Prometheus. Who is this Prometheus and for what does he stand? Perhaps we shall get to know him best through the gifts which he bestowed so liberally on man. These gifts which Prometheus lists in detail for us comprise the whole range of human arts and sciences. All of man's cultural and intellectual activity is based on the gifts of Prometheus. Prometheus, therefore, stands as a symbol of all cultural and intellectual achievement, of all, indeed, that is meant by the word "civilization," for it is the possession of his gifts to mankind that we use as a criterion to distinguish between the civilized and barbarous society. If Zeus, the tyrannical god of nature, can be forced to yield some day to Prometheus, then Aeschylus is telling us, symbolically, that the wild, savage forces of nature can be made to give way to the power of civilization and that man, Prometheus' ward, the proud bearer of Prometheus' gifts, will be the agent for effecting this change.[11]

 11. On this point Solmsen takes an opposed point of view. He writes (*Hesiod and Aeschylus*, p. 145): "In *Prometheus Bound* nothing is said that might bridge the gulf between the two opposite views of man's existence, between the pride of man's achievement and the realization of his helplessness. Each of them is set forth by itself and without any reference to the complementary point of view." However, in presenting in detail the catalogue of Prometheus' gifts to man Aeschylus clearly indicates that the world of man's helplessness and his achievement are not separate entities. It is obvious that the domain of man's helplessness was much greater before he received Prometheus' gifts than afterward, and it is also clear that these gifts have played a continuous role as mediators between the worlds of man's achievement and his helplessness and have significantly increased the one at the expense of the other. Solmsen, however, continues the argument quoted above by saying: "What might mediate between them but is absent is the ethical conception of man, his obligation to practice Justice and to avoid *hybris*, and all the related ideas so familiar to us from Aeschylus' other tragedies in which the choruses—and not only the choruses—dwell on them and emphasize their importance again and again." Yet these conceptions are

Aeschylus' theology now becomes clearer. His Zeus symbolizes the universe and is a summation of the poet's experience of a world in which he saw two opposed tendencies at work. The just and protective Zeus of the *Suppliants* represents the constructive factors in man's situation—religion, morality, law —which are his highest and noblest achievement and which become, themselves, the basis of further steps forward in the history of civilization. The cruel and tyrannical Zeus of the *Prometheus Bound* is the unleashed, uncontrolled brute power of nature which often threatens man. Zeus is Aeschylus' term to describe these great forces that both clearly exist in the world. Since the poet is unable to explain the ultimate first principles of the universe, any more than we can, he gives the name of Zeus to them and this provides at least two advantages. The mere *naming* of an unknown object lessens our estrangement from that object and permits us to speak about it. This, in turn, provides us with an opportunity to express our intuitive insights, our best guesses concerning ineluctable mysteries which, paradoxically, contain no guarantee of their truth and yet represent the highest and most significant achievements of the human spirit. Aeschylus' view of Zeus as a symbol of the totality of forces existing in the world is further refined and made more explicit in the great Zeus hymn of the *Agamemnon* and in analyzing this hymn in the second part of this chapter we will define, more sharply and specifically, Aeschylus' conception of divine power. At present we can say that if we accept Aeschylus' symbolic use of the name "Zeus" to stand for all of the ultimate forces, of society and of nature, that significantly affect us, then we can explain away the apparent

---

the necessary moral background for this play as they are, indeed, for all effective human action. If this were not so then what basis would Solmsen have for saying: "At present both parties are wrong . . . although Prometheus on the strength of his record and in view of his suffering has a greater claim on pity, sympathy, and pardon." If there is anything in Prometheus' record which makes him worthy of pardon, it must be the morality of his position; and if there is anything in Zeus's record which makes him subject to censure, it must be the immorality of his attitude.

contradiction in the poet's concept of Zeus which was the starting point of our analysis. The world, itself, offers evidence for these forces which must be linked with whatever power transcendently guides man to his ultimate goal. Aeschylus recognizes the existence of that power but is unwilling to speak about it except in terms of its visible effects in the world. Weighing and balancing the totality of these visible effects, Aeschylus takes a basically optimistic and hopeful attitude toward the human condition for, although man, in his view, is caught up in the tension between the protective and destructive aspects of Zeus's character, he is not a passive spectator, a plaything of the gods. His principal weapon in this situation is his Promethean intelligence, skill, and knowledge—the great range of arts and sciences bestowed upon him by his divine benefactor—which enables him to affect the outcome of the struggle between the just Zeus who protects and the savage Zeus who destroys. The history of civilization bears important witness in favor of this interpretation of the human situation. When Aeschylus introduced into the play the impressive catalogue of Prometheus' gifts to man he indicated that he knew, just as we know today, of signal examples of the victories that man's intellect has won over a hostile nature.[12]

It therefore becomes evident that Aeschylus' complex Zeus cannot be understood independently of his relationship to man. Man's place in the universe, then, is a large one, for what more brilliant destiny could Aeschylus forge for him than to make him a participant in the cosmic drama, holding in his hands the ultimate decision whether Zeus the Protector or Zeus the Destroyer will prevail in the world? [13]

---

12. G. Thomson, *Aeschylus and Athens* (London, 1941), p. 328, takes a view very close to this when he says, "Intelligence, the gift of Prometheus, had made man free, because it had enabled him to comprehend, and so to control, the laws of nature."

13. This idea of a partnership between man and god is expressed elsewhere by Aeschylus. In the *Oresteia* Apollo and the Erinyes take opposed views on Clytemnestra's murder. It is the grave responsibility of Orestes, with the help of Athena, to choose between the rival claims of these divine forces.

2.

The conception of Zeus which we have observed in our analysis of the *Suppliants* and the *Prometheus Bound* is given its most profound and clearest formulation in the *Agamemnon*. We present our interpretation of the theology of this play both as the climactic statement of the Aeschylean view of Zeus and as a harmonizing line of evidence which supports the conclusions drawn at the end of the first section of this chapter.

In the views of H. W. Smyth which we quoted earlier, we can find positions stated or suggested that have come to be elaborated into the polar oppositions that currently divide, in such radical fashion, interpreters of Aeschylean theology. Smyth, we remember, told us, at one point, of the poet's conception of "the perfectioning of the crude mythological Zeus into the Zeus of a spiritual religion" and then added his description of Aeschylus as "an evolutionist as regards both gods and man." We recall that Smyth also spoke, at another point, of Aeschylus' view of Zeus as a god "ever fluctuating, ever inconsistent" who "for the depiction of character . . . is no more than human."

Smyth's first view, mentioned above, has been elaborated by one group of modern scholars which looks upon Aeschylus' Zeus as a deity who, whatever his original nature may have been, developed ultimately into a god of justice, mercy, and grace. The Zeus envisioned by these scholars resembles very closely the Judaic-Christian concept of God and has a highly developed morality associated with him.[14] This view has been rejected by some of the ablest modern scholars who have directed strong and effective criticism at it. They have shown the lack of any textual evidence for a conversion of Zeus from an obviously cruel and vicious god into one supporting, by his

14. For representative statements of this point of view see A. D. Fitton-Brown, "Prometheia," *JHS*, LXXIX (1959), 52–60; G. Murray, *Aeschylus: The Creator of Tragedy* (Oxford, 1940), pp. 108–10; H. W. Smyth, *Aeschylean Tragedy* (Berkeley, 1924), pp. 120–21; F. Solmsen, *Hesiod and Aeschylus* (Ithaca, 1949), pp. 153–66.

power and grace, an advanced and highly developed morality. They have pointed out specific and very clear evidence for Zeus's cruelty and violence in the *Prometheus Bound* and in the *Oresteia* and have shown that, with the lack of any textual evidence for the conversion or evolution of Zeus, we are required to accept the existence of cruelty and violence as an essential part of Zeus's character.[15] In the absence of any textual evidence and because of the many cogent arguments based on the logic and probability of the situation, we must reject the position of those scholars who make Aeschylus' Zeus resemble the Judaic-Christian concept of God. Smyth's other view that Aeschylus has represented his Zeus as an inconsistent, anthropomorphic deity has been developed by a second group of scholars who connect Aeschylean religious thought with the unsophisticated Hesiodic theology that was current hundreds of years earlier. This hypothesis is the one which is currently most in favor.[16] It conceives of Aeschylus' Zeus not only as primitive and anthropomorphic but as an arbitrary, confused, and self-contradictory deity practicing violence and crime one moment and insisting on the obedience of men and gods to the principles of justice in the next. The scholars who hold this view recognize the petty insignificance to which they have reduced Zeus; and they are forced to justify their interpretation by asserting that, although Aeschylus was a sublime poet and brilliant dramatist, in the field of theology he was merely a backward and naïve thinker.[17]

15. See the persuasive arguments made on this point by both H. Lloyd-Jones, "Zeus in Aeschylus," *JHS*, LXXVI (1956), 57, 66; and K. Reinhardt, *Aischylos als Regisseur und Theologe* (Bern, 1949), pp. 68–76.

16. It is at least the one which has received the most serious recent endorsement. For a particularly eloquent statement of this view see the edition of Aeschylus' *Agamemnon* by J. D. Denniston and D. Page (Oxford, 1957), pp. xii–xvi. See also Lloyd-Jones, "Zeus in Aeschylus," pp. 65–67. I know of no attempt, subsequent to the publication of the views of these scholars, to refute their position.

17. Thus Page, *Agamemnon*, p. xv, writes that, "Aeschylus is first and foremost a great poet and a most powerful dramatist: the faculty of acute or profound thought is not among his gifts."

RELIGIOUS DRAMA   [115]

It is our contention in this chapter that the evidence from the plays in which Zeus figures most prominently, the *Suppliants*, *Prometheus Bound*, and *Agamemnon*, conclusively shows that Aeschylus' actual view of Zeus is different from either of the current standard interpretations. Having discussed the *Suppliants* and the *Prometheus Bound*, we must now assess the evidence from the *Agamemnon* which holds a place of such critical importance in the canon of the poet's work.

Denys Page in the Introduction to his edition of this play presents, in its most recent, influential, and widely disseminated form, the interpretation of the Aeschylean Zeus as a primitive and inconsistent deity. We must, therefore, discuss his arguments, in detail, here. Page speaks of Zeus in general in his Introduction; but as his remarks appear in an edition of the *Agamemnon*, we have every right to expect that they have special reference to the Zeus of this play. Of Aeschylus' general theological attitude Page says the following:

Innumerable superstitions darkened and dominated the lives of men, even among the most intelligent; and in this respect Aeschylus was certainly not in advance of his time. For him, the ministers of the divine will are a diverse and jealous brood, and Zeus appears indifferent to the conflict of their claims. The crime of Orestes was enjoined by Apollo at the command of Zeus; who nevertheless authorized the Furies to exact retribution. Zeus himself commanded Agamemnon to sail to Troy; but looked on with stoical calm while his daughter Artemis prevented Agamemnon from sailing except at the cost of inexpiable crime, the killing of Iphigeneia.[18]

In such a situation Page sees "much that is crude, and much that is confused," and he despairs of finding any kind of coherent theology or philosophy in Aeschylus. Page's interpretation of the essential nature of Aeschylus' Zeus is most clearly given by him in the following words:

We must be on our guard against the temptation to believe that his gods and demons are represented as being laws or forces

18. *Ibid.*, pp. xiv-xv.

of a spiritual kind; in truth he gives them human shape and many human qualities. All, except Zeus, may walk on earth, and all may be manifest to human sight. We are told that they have eyes to see and ears to hear; what clothes they wear, and by what means they travel. Zeus himself has human shape, is seated on a throne in a palace like a mortal tyrant; has bow and arrows, weighs in actual scales. Even he was once a character in an Aeschylean play.[19]

Thus for Page, Aeschylus is a superstitious and naïve thinker who believes in a primitive and anthropomorphic Zeus. The immediate problem with Page's analysis is that no specific textual evidence is cited to justify this position. In the Preface to his edition of the *Agamemnon*, however, Page acknowledges the co-operation of several other scholars in developing the views of Aeschylean theology that are presented in his Introduction. In the published work of one of these co-operating scholars, H. Lloyd-Jones, specific textual evidence for certain anthropomorphic characteristics of Zeus is given.[20] The similarity in thought that is evident between the statements made on this subject by Lloyd-Jones and Page clearly indicates that it was the evidence assembled by the former scholar which Page drew on to support his interpretation of Aeschylus' conception of Zeus.[21] Lloyd-Jones substantiates his view that Aeschylus had a primitive, anthropomorphic notion of Zeus by citing certain passages which indicate that the gods have human form, which describe the ways in which they travel and which tell us the weapons they use in battle. One highly significant fact emerges, however, from an examination of the passages he cites. None of these passages comes from the

19. *Ibid.*, p. xv.
20. Lloyd-Jones, "Zeus in Aeschylus," p. 65.
21. Page uses exactly the same categories of anthropomorphic qualities which Lloyd-Jones employs: references to the bodily form of the gods, to their means of transportation, and to the weapons they use. Both scholars make the same point about Zeus's appearance in a play and both contrast Aeschylean theology with the ideas of Xenophanes and Heracleitus. Since their thought on these points is so similar and since Page acknowledges Lloyd-Jones's contribution in his Preface, we may assume that Page's judgments rest, at least in large measure, on the same evidence as that assembled by Lloyd-Jones.

RELIGIOUS DRAMA   [117]

Agamemnon.²² Page's interpretation of the Zeus of the *Agamemnon* as an anthropomorphic deity is open to question since neither he nor Lloyd-Jones cites any textual evidence in support of it from the play itself. It therefore becomes necessary for us to undertake a detailed and thorough review of the evidence bearing on Zeus in the *Agamemnon* to see exactly what conception of this god Aeschylus actually had.

A reading of the text of the play shows that it contains twenty-two references to Zeus. An analysis of these references yields important information which is not in accord with current interpretations of Aeschylus' theology.

Almost the entire body of references to Zeus in this play, some twenty in number, identify him with some physical or spiritual force in the world. Thus there are references to Zeus as an agricultural deity responsible for the ripening of crops and for the fruitfulness of the earth (970, 1014). There are references to Zeus as the guardian of specific moral and spiritual qualities. For example, he is described as the bringer of justice and retribution against transgressors of the moral order (58–59, 526); he is described as the protector of the rights of hospitality (61–62, 362, 748) and as the defender of the hearth (704). Most, however, of the twenty references to Zeus as a force in the universe describe him simply as a god

22. Even the few passages which Lloyd-Jones, "Zeus in Aeschylus," p. 65, notes 35 and 36, cites from other plays of Aeschylus are subject to a reasonable metaphorical interpretation instead of the literal one which he makes. To speak of the weapons or even the parts of the body of one's gods is not necessarily to believe in their literal existence. The concept of deity is so august, supreme, and infinite that it is only through metaphor and symbol that man with his finite intellect can apprehend it. Thus in the famous American Civil War hymn, *The Battle Hymn of the Republic*, we find the following lines: "Mine eyes have seen the glory of the coming of the Lord;/He is trampling out the vintage where the grapes of wrath are stored;/He hath loosed the fateful lightning of His terrible, swift sword;/His truth is marching on." I think that not very many of those who have sung these lines have been compelled to take them literally. The lines are clearly metaphorical and vividly indicate divine power. It will be argued in this chapter that the references to the parts of the body or the weapons of the gods in Aeschylus are precisely of this type and there is significant evidence that they are not meant to be taken literally.

who accomplishes all of the visible effects in the world. Thus the chorus and the herald honor Zeus as the source of the victory at Troy and of the safe return of the army (355–66, 509, 581–82);[23] the chorus declares Zeus to be the source of royal power (43) as well as of that power which prevents the dead from returning to life (1018–24); the source of human fortune and misfortune is traced back to Zeus (367, 1036, 1424)[24] as is the source of that power by which man extricates himself from difficulties (677). All of these indications of Zeus as the accomplishing force in the universe are clearly and unequivocally confirmed by the epithets which herald Zeus as the "Accomplisher" (973) and as "The Cause of all, the Doer of All" (1486). The confirmation of this view of Zeus reaches its culmination in the rhetorical questions asked by the chorus: "For what is accomplished for men without Zeus? What of these things is not divinely ordained?" (1487–88) These questions clarify the meaning of the words spoken earlier by the chorus in honor of Zeus (160–84). The Zeus worshipped somewhat mysteriously in those lines is now clearly seen as the ultimate causal agent in the universe. The tracing back of all of the proximate causes of human actions and natural events leads to a mysterious first cause that is beyond the ability of the human intellect to apprehend. This first cause the chorus is willing to call "Zeus, whatever its name may be"; and it is clear that the Zeus who is described in these terms is an impersonal force or power who is in no sense represented in anthropomorphic terms.

A highly significant point about this force or power which we call Zeus is that he is invoked with equal sincerity by the chorus, who call upon him to protect the conventional moral

---

23. The reference to Zeus as the "highest of the land" at line 509 is a fairly general one. The context in which it occurs shows, however, that the herald is thinking about his safe return home, and his invocation of Zeus and Apollo indicates his feeling that they are responsible for this last piece of good fortune after all the suffering they imposed upon him at Troy.

24. The reference in line 1424 is literally to *theos* who is, in the context, most easily and clearly understood to be Zeus.

order, and by Clytemnestra, who begs him to assist her in the crime of murdering her husband (973). This clearly indicates that the force Zeus represents is neither moral nor immoral but, rather, amoral. Zeus is simply force, whatever accomplishes, whatever has an effect. He is in the very words of the chorus the "Cause of All" and the "Doer of All."

Twenty of the twenty-two references to Zeus in the *Agamemnon* fit into the categories discussed above and do not admit, as we have shown, of an anthropomorphic interpretation. There are, however, two references to Zeus in this play which, although they are not mentioned by Lloyd-Jones, are open to a possible anthropomorphic interpretation. The first of these occurs at line 469, where it is indicated that a thunderbolt is hurled by Zeus at those who prosper excessively. The second occurs at line 1563 and tells us that the law "the doer must suffer" will remain in force as long as Zeus remains on his throne. These two references so different in character from all of the others in the play are the only textual evidence that Page can cite from the *Agamemnon* itself to justify his view that Aeschylus' Zeus is an anthropomorphic deity.[25] Even here, however, we are entitled to register some objections to

25. In this regard we must mention an extremely important reference to Zeus at line 362 ff. where he, as we have already seen, is described as the protector of the rights of hospitality. The chorus goes on to tell us that Zeus had for a long time stretched his bow against Alexander. Here, indeed, is a reference to a bow, but it is not one which, I think, Page could cite in support of his anthropomorphic view of Aeschylus' Zeus. In fact it is the strongest possible evidence against his position. The reference to the bow comes immediately after night has been described as having hurled a net over Troy. The net of night and the bow of Zeus are parallel metaphors, and there is no warrant for taking one more literally than the other. We also know, clearly, that the actual agents involved in the destroying of Troy and punishing of Paris were Agamemnon and his army. Thus Zeus's bow must be a metaphor for the destructive forces that were unleashed against Troy. Since we have here a clear and indisputable example of an anthropomorphic quality being used in a metaphorical sense, I do not include it in the same category as the other possibly anthropomorphic references to Zeus discussed in this paragraph. Because of the clear metaphorical character of this reference to Zeus's bow we should be wary of accepting a literal interpretation of similar expressions elsewhere in Aeschylus.

considering the thunderbolt and throne images as actually anthropomorphic in character. In the diction of any poet we find the use of highly imaginative and metaphorical language. In the *Agamemnon* many vivid examples of such diction can be found. I should like to cite here three illustrative examples:

> ξυνώμοσαν γάρ, ὄντες ἔχθιστοι τὸ πρίν,
> πῦρ καὶ θάλασσα, καὶ τὰ πίστ' ἐδειξάτην
> φθείροντε τὸν δύστηνον 'Αργείων στρατόν   (650-52)

(*Although they had previously been enemies, fire and water formed an alliance and offered pledges for it by destroying the wretched Argive army*)

> εἰ δ' οὖν τις ἀκτὶς ἡλίου νιν ἱστορεῖ
> χλωρόν τε καὶ βλέποντα   (676-77)

(*If, then, some ray of the sun seeks him out still living and breathing*)

> δαίμονος χηλῇ βαρείᾳ δυστυχῶς πεπληγμένοι   (1660)

(*miserably struck by the heavy hoof of the daemon*).

Certainly no critic would argue for a literal interpretation of any of the above lines. No one would accuse Aeschylus of literally believing that fire and water could conclude an alliance, or that the rays of the sun could "seek out" a person in any but a metaphorical sense, or that he envisioned demons as oxen with heavy hoofs trampling on miserable human beings. It is clearly the very essence of the poet's art to interpret reality in metaphorical terms. If we grant the poet's right to speak of the sun and the sea in metaphorical terms, then we must also recognize the possibility of his speaking of Zeus and the other gods in these terms.[26] The thunderbolt is a

26. There is only one major incident in the *Agamemnon* in which we have an actual example of anthropomorphic activity on the part of the gods. This concerns the description given by Cassandra of her seduction by Apollo. This incident is part of the mythical background of the play, just as many of the details of the expedition against Troy are part of a traditional story upon which Aeschylus drew for this play. The story of Cassandra and Apollo was one, therefore, to which an audience steeped

vivid symbol for divine vengeance, and the description of Zeus remaining on his throne is a poetic way of expressing the notion of the duration of divine power. When we recall that these two images are used in the general context of some twenty clearly non-anthropomorphic references to Zeus, we have considerable justification for considering them to be nothing more than metaphors of the type used by the poet regularly throughout the play.

Thus we have established that there is no adequate evidence supporting the view that the Zeus of the *Agamemnon* is a primitive, anthropomorphic deity. The evidence for anthropomorphism which Page used, we have seen, comes exclusively from plays other than the *Agamemnon*. In the *Agamemnon*, itself, contrary to what Page says in his Introduction, nothing whatever is stated about Zeus's human form, his mode of travel, his appearance to human sight, his clothes, his use of actual scales, or his possession of a bow and arrows. A bow is, indeed, mentioned at line 364 but in an indisputably metaphorical sense which contradicts rather than supports Page's anthropomorphic interpretation of Aeschylus' Zeus.[27] The two references to Zeus's thunderbolt and his throne have been cited, and their probable metaphorical character has been discussed. In re-evaluating the evidence from the *Agamemnon* itself we have seen that twenty of the twenty-two references to Zeus in the play are entirely devoid of anthropomorphic content and simply describe Zeus as that force or power which accomplishes all of the visible effects in the universe.

Aeschylus' Zeus thus turns out to be a very different type of deity from the primitive, anthropomorphic god posited by Page and others. We have seen that the Zeus of the *Agamemnon* is regularly identified as the force that is ultimately

in the traditional legend might well have expected some reference. This incident, however, is totally irrelevant to the principal theological problems explored in the *Oresteia*, which deal with the complicated fate of the House of Atreus. Cassandra is involved tragically, but only incidentally, in the major theme of the play. Thus the story of Apollo's relationship to Cassandra does not have any central significance in the major theological problems raised by the events in the *Oresteia*.

27. See the discussion in note 25 above.

responsible for the occurrence of all events in the world. Let us take any situation which might happen. It may be a bountiful crop, a safe return from war, or the murder of a husband by a wife. In the *Agamemnon* Zeus is held ultimately responsible for all of these events. Now these occurrences have proximate causes which are usually quite clear to the human intellect. The chain of causes and effects, however, when pursued further back ultimately recedes into mystery, at least as far as human intelligence goes. The ultimate cause of any event is forever eluding the mind of man, but nevertheless he, almost of necessity, maintains a faith in it. Zeus fulfills the function of ultimate cause for Aeschylus, and his belief in such a cause is summed up by the chorus of the *Agamemnon* in the line "What without Zeus is accomplished for man?" Since the limitations on man's reason forbid him to know the essential nature of this ultimate cause, all that man can do is to recognize its existence by naming it. It is in this sense that we are to understand the lines:

> Ζεύς, ὅστις ποτ' ἐστίν, εἰ τόδ' αὐ-
> τῷ φίλον κεκλημένῳ,
> τοῦτό νιν προσεννέπω.
> οὐκ ἔχω προσεικάσαι
> πάντ' ἐπισταθμώμενος
> πλὴν Διός, εἰ τὸ μάταν ἀπὸ φροντίδος ἄχθος
> χρὴ βαλεῖν ἐτητύμως.[28] (160–66)

(*Zeus, whoever he is, if it pleases him to be called by this name, by this name do I address him. Although I have pondered everything, I am unable to compare him to anyone, except Zeus, if I am, truly, to cast this vain burden from my mind*).

Thus the chorus expresses its faith in an ultimate power in the universe and attaches a name to it by which it may address and

---

28. For a highly perceptive and profound interpretation of the meaning of the phrase "Zeus, whoever he is . . . ," see E. Fraenkel (*Agamemnon* [Oxford, 1950], 2. 99–100). Fraenkel's interpretation, with which I am in agreement, appears to me to be in much closer harmony with Aeschylus' conception of Zeus than the interpretation of this passage given by Lloyd-Jones, "Zeus in Aeschylus," pp. 61–62.

approach it. The "vain burden" referred to by the chorus may easily be understood as the fruitless search for an ultimate cause by the limited human intellect.[29] The naming of Zeus puts an end to this fruitless search. Substantiating proof for this view of the chorus' attitude toward Zeus may be found in their reference to him already quoted, at line 1486, as the "Cause of All" and "Doer of All." In this sense, then, Zeus is a spiritual conception in that he symbolizes all of the effecting, all of the accomplishing forces in the universe. To say, however, that he is portrayed as a spiritual force is not in any sense to assert that he represents an advanced morality of the Judaic-Christian type.[30] The fact that Clytemnestra can, with utter sincerity,

29. For a perceptive, but differing, analysis of the meaning of the term "vain burden," see again Fraenkel, *Agamemnon*, pp. 102-3.

30. The concept of Zeus as a spiritual force has been advanced by other scholars. M. P. Nilsson, *Geschichte der griechischen Religion* 1 (München, 1941), 711, writes, "Oft werden die Allmacht und die Gerechtigkeit des Zeus gemeinsam verherrlicht; er vollzieht die ausgleichende Gerechtigkeit, er wird als derjenige bezeichnet, der alles bewirkt. Seine Macht wird so gesteigert, dass er an einer Stelle mehr als ein Prinzip denn als ein persönlicher Gott erscheint." H. D. F. Kitto, in a paper appearing in *La notion du divin depuis Homère jusqu' à Platon* (Geneva, 1952), p. 188, interprets Aeschylus' Zeus as "the spirit of progress." While this is a spiritual interpretation of Zeus, it fails to recognize and account for the patently destructive and harmful aspects of Zeus's character that are clearly pointed out in the *Oresteia* and in the *Prometheus Bound*. Associated with the question of the spiritual quality of Zeus is the question of monotheism. The case for a monotheistic interpretation of Zeus is stated by H. J. Rose, *A Handbook of Greek Literature* (London, 1956), p. 159, who writes, "Practically, Aeschylus was a monotheist, not that he denied the existence of other deities, for we may gather that quite apart from mythology he was ready enough to admit the reality of such beings as Athena or Apollo, but that he subordinates all else to Zeus, including the gods who were before him, Uranos and Kronos." In the *Agamemnon*, with the sole exception of the story of Apollo's seduction of Cassandra which has already been discussed, the lesser gods are referred to as symbols of power in the same way as Zeus is. See, for example, lines 55-56. Thus the concept of divinity appears to be for Aeschylus the concept of power. There are many limited expressions of this power in one direction or area, and these are symbolized by the names of the Olympian gods who are subordinate to Zeus. Unlimited, ultimate, primal power which is the first cause of all things is, however, symbolized by the name Zeus. The equation of ultimate power with Zeus is, indeed, as Rose points out, the equivalent, in practical terms, of monotheism.

invoke the aid of Zeus in accomplishing her crime has already been cited as significant evidence against this point of view. On the contrary, Zeus is a name used to symbolize all of the forces of the universe whether they accomplish moral or immoral ends from man's point of view. The Zeus of Aeschylus is an impersonal, amoral force representing universal power in its fullest, most naked form. Whatever happens in the world, moral or immoral, must ultimately be traced back to Zeus the Accomplisher.

Zeus understood in this way, as the name attached to that power which accomplishes its purposes, which works its inevitable effects in the universe, is freed from the contradictory, puzzling, and absurd behavior which the anthropomorphic interpretation imposes upon him. In a passage quoted earlier in this paper Page pointed out the enigmatic and self-contradictory actions of Zeus in regard to the events of the *Agamemnon*. If these actions are considered as the product of a mind analogous to, although greater than, the human mind, then they are, of course, absurd and self-contradictory; and the god identified with them must share in their absurdity. If, however, Zeus is understood as a symbol of the ultimate cause of all events in the world, then we have a sophisticated conception of deity that is free from absurdity and self-contradiction.

If we understand Zeus in this way, then we can understand more fully the highly significant point made by Aeschylus in the *Oresteia* about the relationship of man to god. In the *Agamemnon*, as Page so well points out, Zeus is at odds with himself, sometimes inciting an action and then bringing retribution to bear on the doer of that action. The various gods take different sides in the play, and every human agent can call on some god for support for his actions. The moral atmosphere surrounding the play is chaotic, and the actions of the gods complicate rather than undo the chaos. In the court scene of the *Eumenides*, however, Aeschylus does provide a solution for the complicated moral problems raised in the *Oresteia*. It is of the utmost importance that we understand the nature of

Aeschylus' solution if we are to understand his real attitude to the gods. In the *Eumenides* Aeschylus describes the establishment of a court to settle the complex questions of guilt and innocence raised by the history of the House of Atreus. It is highly significant that the court which is to decide a question that Zeus himself and the whole race of Olympian gods are unable to settle is composed of a group of human beings under the guardianship of Athena. A human court under the protection of a goddess who, if we look at her symbolically rather than literally, represents wisdom and understanding is to settle the moral questions which have eluded solution by the gods.[31] This human court is, furthermore, to have in its power for all future time the authority to make decisions in matters of this type. I submit that if Aeschylus were a naïve, primitive religious thinker, he would never have authorized the transfer of the authority for solving difficult moral problems from the gods to a human agency relying on reason and wisdom. Aeschylus' solution as given here actually heralds the breakdown of naïve religious thought. It places in the hands of man the ultimate responsibility of deciding moral questions in human society while recognizing the existence of an ultimate divine cause of all events in the world. It is a solution, also, that is in harmony with the action of the *Prometheus Bound* where it is predicted that Zeus, who symbolizes the totality of power in the universe, must eventually yield to Prometheus who represents the forces of human intellect and civilization. The symbolism of that play indicates that man, the recipient of Prometheus' civilizing gifts, can use them to influence the way in which the protective and destructive forces represented by Zeus affect his life. In the *Oresteia* and the *Prometheus Bound* Aeschylus has elevated man to a position of full responsibility for his actions and for the judgment of his actions, thus emancipating him from a naïve dependence on the unclear and manifestly self-contradictory will of the gods.

31. In the *Eumenides* Athena declares at lines 470 ff. that the affair is too great for her to settle by herself, and she summons the aid of a human court.

Page has, however, written as follows of Aeschylus' theology: "Nowhere is there any awareness of what profounder thinkers had been preaching for many years: reading the meagre fragments of Xenophanes and Heracleitus, we should naturally suppose that Aeschylus must have lived long before them, so much more penetrating is their insight into the nature of the world and the mind of man." [32]

On the basis of the evidence cited in this book we may take exception to this evaluation of Aeschylus' religious thought.[33]

Now, like the shepherd who comes to unravel the mystery of Oedipus' birth, I am on the verge of saying fearful words—certainly they are highly unorthodox ones. Aeschylus clearly emerges from this analysis not as a naïve, primitive religious thinker but rather as a humanist, a rationalist, and as an eminently fitting companion to the great minds who stamped fifth-century Athens with its unique, unquenchable brilliance. Aeschylus' humanism is seen in the emphasis he places on human responsibility for action and judgment in the *Oresteia* and in the *Prometheus Bound*. His rationalism and his sophisticated thought are seen in his intellectual conception of Zeus as an impersonal force governing the universe who is known to us only by the effects he produces in the world. Beyond the fact that Zeus is the ultimate cause of all events which occur in the world, Aeschylus does not attempt to tell us much, if anything, about his nature. Perhaps, however, he has told us all that can be told in the majestic hymn chanted to Zeus by the chorus early in the play: "Zeus, whoever he is, if it please him to be called by this name, by this name do I address him" (160–162).

32. Page, *Agamemnon*, p. xv.
33. For views and evidence opposed to Page's interpretation, see B. Gladigow, "Aischylos und Heraklit," *Archiv für Geschichte der Philosophie*, N.S. XLIV (1962), 225–39 and W. Jaeger, *Die Theologie der frühen griechischen Denker* (Stuttgart, 1953), p. 58.

CONCLUSION

THE ACHIEVEMENT
OF AESCHYLUS

AS THE FIRST CLEAR FIGURE SET AGAINST THE MISTY BACKGROUND of early Greek drama, Aeschylus has always loomed large as a poet of supreme importance in the process of bringing fifth-century tragedy to formal perfection. If he had accomplished no more than to be the principal shaper of a significant literary genre, his immortality in cultural history would be assured. Clearly his achievement is far greater than that. Aeschylus gazed into the heart of the mystery of man's existence and saw there the grand, humanistic vision which infuses his greatest work, the vision of an ever-continuing progress forged by the power of the human intellect. This idea proudly illuminates the *Prometheus Bound* where the poet heralds the science and technology that man uses to tame and mold nature to his benefit and the *Oresteia* where he proclaims the sophisticated principles of law and morality that are the basis of a highly developed civilization.

It is Prometheus, then, and not a primitive Zeus nor a warlike Ares, who hovers benignly, optimistically, and triumphantly over Aeschylus' work and provides, as the essential theme of the poet's song, the marvels wrought by the mind of man.

BIBLIOGRAPHY
OF WORKS CITED

Adcock, F. E. *Cambridge Ancient History*. Vol. IV Cambridge: 1960.
Blomfield, C. J. *Aeschyli Persae*. London: 1840.
Broadhead, H. D. *The Persae of Aeschylus*. Cambridge: 1960.
Burgess, T. C. *Epideictic Literature*. Chicago: 1902.
Cherniss, H. "The Biographical Fashion in Literary Criticism," *University of California Publications in Classical Philology*, XII (1933–44), 279–91.
Denniston, J. D., and D. Page. *Aeschylus: Agamemnon*. Oxford: 1957.
Dodds, E. R. *The Greeks and the Irrational*. Berkeley: 1951.
———. *Humanism and Technique in Greek Studies*. Oxford: 1936.
———. "Morals and Politics in the *Oresteia*," *Proceedings of the Cambridge Philological Society*, N.S. VI (1960), 19–31.
Farrington, B. *Greek Science*. Baltimore: 1953.
Finley, J. H., Jr. *Pindar and Aeschylus*. Cambridge, Mass.: 1955.
Fitton-Brown, A. D. "Prometheia," *Journal of Hellenic Studies*, LXXIX (1959), 52–60.

Fraenkel, E. *Aeschylus: Agamemnon.* 3 vols. Oxford: 1950.
Fritz, Kurt von. *Antike und moderne Tragödie.* Berlin: 1962, pp. 193–226.
Gladigow, B. "Aischylos und Heraklit," *Archiv für Geschichte der Philosophie,* N.S. XLIV (1962), 225–39.
Gomme, A. W. "The Position of Women in Athens in the Fifth and Fourth Centuries," *Classical Philology,* XX (1925), 1–25.
Groeneboom, P. *Aischylos' Perser.* Göttingen: 1960.
Hölzle, R. *Zum Aufbau der lyrischen Partien des Aischylos.* Marbach a.N.: 1934.
Jaeger, W. "Classical Philology and Humanism," *Transactions of the American Philological Association,* LXVII (1936), 363–74.
———. *Paideia.* 3 vols. New York: 1945.
———. *Die Theologie der frühen griechischen Denker.* Stuttgart: 1953.
Jones, J. *On Aristotle and Greek Tragedy.* New York: 1962.
Kaufmann-Bühler, D. *Begriff und Funktion der Dike in den Tragödien des Aischylos.* Bonn: 1955.
Kennedy, G. *The Art of Persuasion in Greece.* Princeton: 1963.
Kitto, H. D. F. *Greek Tragedy.* London: 1950.
———. "The Idea of God in Aeschylus and Sophocles," in *La notion du divin depuis Homère jusque' à Platon.* Geneva: 1952, pp. 169–89.
Klotz, O. "Zu Aischylos' thebanischer Tetralogie," *Rheinisches Museum,* LXXII (1917–18), 616–25.
Lattimore, R. "Aeschylus on the Defeat of Xerxes," in *Classical Studies in Honor of William Abbott Oldfather.* Urbana: 1943, pp. 82–93.
Lesky, A. "Eteokles in den *Sieben gegen Theben*," *Wiener Studien,* LXXIV (1961), 5–17.
Lloyd-Jones, H. "The End of the *Seven against Thebes*," *Classical Quarterly,* N.S. IX (1959), 80–115.
———. "The Guilt of Agamemnon," *Classical Quarterly,* XII (1962), 187–99.
———. "Zeus in Aeschylus," *Journal of Hellenic Studies,* LXXVI (1956), 55–67.

Murray, G. *Aeschylus: The Creator of Tragedy*. Oxford: 1940.
Nilsson, M.P. *Geschichte der griechischen Religion*. 2 vols. München: 1941.
Otis, B. "The Unity of the *Seven Against Thebes*," *Greek, Roman, and Byzantine Studies*, III (1960), 153-74.
Patzer, H. "Die dramatische Handlung der *Sieben gegen Theben*," *Harvard Studies in Classical Philology*, LXIII (1958), 97-119.
Regenbogen, O. "Humanism—heute?" in *Kleine Schriften*. München: 1961, pp. 463-79.
Reinhardt, K. *Aischylos als Regisseur und Theologe*. Bern: 1949.
Rose, H. J. *A Handbook of Greek Literature*. London: 1956.
Rosenmeyer, T. G. *The Masks of Tragedy: Essays on Six Greek Dramas*. Austin: 1963.
Sidgwick, A. *Aeschylus: Agamemnon*. Oxford: 1925.
———. *Aeschylus: Eumenides*. Oxford: 1927.
———. *Aeschylus: Persae*. Oxford: 1903.
———. *Aeschylus: Septem contra Thebas*. Oxford: 1903.
Smyth, H. W. *Aeschylean Tragedy*. Berkeley: 1924.
Solmsen, F. "The Erinys in Aischylos' *Septem*," *Transactions of the American Philological Association*, LXVIII (1937), 197-211.
———. *Hesiod and Aeschylus*. Ithaca: 1949.
Thomson, G. *Aeschylus and Athens*. London: 1941.
Tucker, T. G. *The "Seven Against Thebes" of Aeschylus*. Cambridge: 1908.
Wilamowitz-Moellendorff, U. von. *Aischylos: Interpretationen*. Berlin: 1914.
Winnington-Ingram, R. P. "Clytemnestra and the Vote of Athena," *Journal of Hellenic Studies*, LXVIII (1948), 130-47.
Wolff, E. "Die Entscheidung des Eteokles in den *Sieben gegen Theben*," *Harvard Studies in Classical Philology*, LXIII (1958), 89-95.

INDEX

INDEX

A

Adcock, F. E., 16
Aegisthus, in the *Agamemnon*, 76–77, 78; in the *Choephoroe*, 81, 83, 85, 86
Agamemnon, 34, 41, 66–98 *passim*
Agamemnon, 8, 43, 62–82, 87, 111, 113–26. See also *Oresteia*
Anaxagoras, 95
Antigone, 51, 52, 55, 56
Apollo, in the *Oresteia*, 61, 88–96 *passim*, 120 n; in the *Oedipus Tyrannus*, 109
Ares, 61, 127
Aristotle, 21, 31, 41, 52 n
Athena, 11, 61, 89–98 *passim*, 125
Atossa, 33–41 *passim*

B

Bia, 107
Blood vengeance, 11, 15, 16, 81–87 *passim*, 92, 93, 94, 98
Book of Job, 106
Broadhead, H. D., on plot development in the *Persians*, 31, 35, 36; on character portrayal in the *Persians*, 33, 34

C

Capture of Miletus, 41
Cassandra, 70, 72, 73, 120 n
Cherniss, H., on the relevance of Classical literature, 28–30
Choephoroe, 43, 75, 79–87. See also *Oresteia*
Chorus, in the *Seven*, 12, 46–51 *passim*; in the *Persians*, 34, 36; in the *Suppliants*, 42, 100, 101, 107 n; in the *Agamemnon*, 66–78 *passim*, 118, 123; in the *Choephoroe*, 80–86 *passim*; in the *Prometheus Bound*, 101
Cleisthenes, 16
Clytemnestra, in the *Agamemnon*, 34, 41, 63–79 *passim*, 119, 123–24; in the *Choephoroe*, 80–86 *passim*; in the *Eumenides*, 88–98 *passim*
Council of the Areopagus, 11, 12, 61, 93, 96, 98
Cratos, 107

INDEX

D

Danaids, See Chorus, in the Suppliants
Darius, 33–41 passim
Dodds, E. R., on Aeschylean theology, 4–5, 13; on the relevance of Classical literature, 26–28, 30
Draco, 15–16

E

Egyptians, 42, 43
Electra, 75, 79, 80, 81, 82
Epideictic oratory, 37–40
Epideictic tragedy, 40, 41
Epigoni, 57, 58, 59, 60
Erinyes, 8–13 passim, 81–98 passim
Eteocles, 8–12 passim, 34, 43–60, 63, 74, 76
Eumenides, 9, 11, 15, 43, 61, 63, 79, 81, 87–99, 124, 125. See also Oresteia

F

Family curse, in the Seven, 12, 49–53 passim, 58, 59, 60; in the Oresteia, 74, 75, 76, 84, 85
Farrington, B., 18–19
Funeral oration, 38, 39, 40. See Epideictic oratory

G

Gladigow, B., 16, 17, 126 n
Gomme, A. W., 22–24
Guard, in the Agamemnon, 64, 65

H

Helen, 74
Hephaestus, 101, 107
Heracleitus, 16, 126
Herald, in the Seven, 55; in the Agamemnon, 68, 118
Hermes, 89, 102
Hesiod, 114

I

Io, 102, 106, 107
Iphigeneia, 73, 75
Ismene, 51, 52, 53, 54, 60

J

Jaeger, W., on Aeschylean theology, 4, 16, 17; on the relevance of Classical literature, 25–26, 30

K

Kennedy, G., 37–38
Klotz, O., 57, 58, 59, 60
Kronos, 105

L

Lloyd-Jones, H., on Aeschylean theology, 8, 116, 117, 119; on the interpretation of the Seven, 55–59

M

Messenger, in the Persians, 34
Metaphorical language, Aeschylus' use of, 120
Murray, G., on Aeschylean theology, 104, 106

N

Nurse, in the Choephoroe, 83, 84

O

Oceanids, 101
Oceanus, 107
Oedipus Tyrannus, 106
Oresteia, 13, 19, 36, 55, 61, 62, 63, 78, 79, 85, 86, 88, 124, 125, 126, 127. See also Agamemnon, Choephoroe and Eumenides
Orestes, 11, 75, 79–97 passim

P

Page, D. L., on Aeschylean theology, 3–4, 8, 13, 16, 115–26 passim
Patriotism, as a theme in Aeschylus, 14, 15, 31–41, 62, 80, 88, 98
Patzer, H., 44, 45, 46
Pelasgus, king of Argos, 42–43, 80
Pericles, 38, 39, 40, 109
Persians, 14, 15, 31–41
Phoenissae, 41
Phrynichus, 41

INDEX

Pisistratus, 15
Plato, 16
Polynices, 50–60 *passim*
Pre-Socratics, 14–15, 16, 95
Prometheus, 19, 34, 41, 89, 100–10 *passim*, 125
Prometheus Bound, 12, 19, 36, 89, 94, 100–13 *passim*, 125, 127
Pylades, 84

R

Rational humanism, in Aeschylean thought, 17, 126, 127

S

Scientific and technological progress, as a theme in Aeschylus, 15, 16, 110–12, 127
Seven against Thebes, 8–14 *passim*, 42–61, 62, 74
Shield scene, in the *Seven*, 53–54
Sidgwick, A., on character portrayal in the *Persians*, 32, 33, 34; on plot development in the *Persians*, 36
Smyth, H. W., on Aeschylus' view of Zeus, 102, 103–4, 113
Social and legal institutions, as a theme in Aeschylus, 14, 15, 16, 19, 42, 43, 60–61, 62, 87–98, 127
Solmsen, F., on Aeschylus' conception of the Erinyes, 8–12 *passim*, 44; mentioned, 58, 59, 60

Solon, 15, 16
Sophocles, 106, 109
Suppliants, 35, 36, 42, 80, 100–13 *passim*

T

Thucydides, 109

V

Von Fritz, K., 45, 46

W

Wilamowitz-Moellendorff, U. von, on plot development in the *Persians*, 5 n, 32; on plot development in the *Seven*, 5 n, 44, 57, 59, 60
Wolff, E., 44

X

Xenophanes, 16, 126
Xerxes, 32–41 *passim*

Z

Zeus, Aeschylus' conception of, 8, 13, 100–27 *passim*; in the *Agamemnon*, 72, 114–25 *passim*; in the *Choephoroe*, 79; in the *Prometheus Bound*, 89, 100–10, 114, 115; in the *Suppliants*, 100–10, 115; mentioned, 91, 95, 97

www.ingramcontent.com/pod-product-compliance
Lightning Source LLC
Chambersburg PA
CBHW030115010526
44116CB00005B/257